D0753604

Supplication

Supplication : selected poems of John Wieners

33305234290629

4an   2/9/16

Supplication
Selected Poems
of John Wieners

Edited by
Joshua Beckman,
CAConrad, and
Robert Dewhurst

Wave Books

Seattle/New York

Published by Wave Books

www.wavepoetry.com

Copyright © 2015 John Wieners Literary Trust, Raymond Foye, Administrator

Compilation copyright © 2015 by Joshua Beckman, CAConrad, and Robert Dewhurst

All rights reserved

Wave Books titles are distributed to the trade by

Consortium Book Sales and Distribution

Phone: 800-283-3572 / SAN 631-760X

Library of Congress Cataloging-in-Publication Data

Wieners, John, 1934–2002.

[Poems. Selections]

Supplication : selected poems of John Wieners / edited by

Joshua Beckman, CAConrad, and Robert Dewhurst. — First edition.

pages ; cm

Includes index.

ISBN 978-1-940696-18-8 (hardcover) — ISBN 978-1-940696-19-5 (softcover)

I. Beckman, Joshua, 1971–, editor. II. Conrad, C. A., editor.

III. Dewhurst, Robert, editor. IV. Title.

PS3573.I35A6 2015

811'.54—dc23

2014047489

Designed and composed by Quemadura

Frontispiece illustration of John Wieners by Robert LaVigne, June 18, 1958. Appears in
the first edition of *The Hotel Wentley Poems*. Used with permission. "About Himself . . ."
John Wieners, handwritten manuscript, c. 1984. John Wieners Papers, Archives and
Special Collections at the Thomas J. Dodd Research Center, University of Connecticut
Libraries. Used with permission of the Estate of John Wieners.

Printed in the United States of America

9 8 7 6 5 4 3 2 1

First Edition

- -

- -

Supplication

With Mr. J. R. Morton

For our nerves
this drink, a beating
on our nerves
no shakedown our heads
but of our nerves

I wish I was a dancer
and cd. move
in feet/undo my body

swing it out it
bangs my bubbs and belly
slide my toes in pebbles so
my nerves
wd. be taken up one by
one stretched out
tight thin to threads
and I wd. be free
inside my legs. My head
not snapped by a King Porter stomp
or played like
Jelly Roll
bends.

Ah daddy I wanna be drunk many days.
On a stage in front of beautiful eyes
I wd. remove my rags,
my dress drop
to work the curtain,
to dance out softly
(over their heads) barefoot on wood
softly
toes like vaseline
knee dips as I strip out my—
I desire to be taken to the top of the Liberty Bell and blown

by winds from Sweden
softly and my toes would do it if I
were a dancer.

Not Complete Enough

How my Mother's embroidered apron unfolds in my life
ARSHILE GORKY

As I put out my cigarette tonight in bed
  I thought of my mother,
    how she would lie
              in the dark
    her bed and as a boy I wd
                open
  the open and see the red spot in her hands.

  I thought of my mother tonight
        when I put out my cigarette
    in the dark bed,
      stomping it out
                and her in
        how I would open the door at night
        and see the red thing in her hands,
          and now a man
          I have the red thing
            and it is the last thing
          I do.
              The last thought that
        the house is clean,
          was her thought mine
        tonight in her home,

red thought
the two of us in the dark,
thoughts of the day,
the clock right, the window open,

how many lunches made,
my life so apart

And yet in her hands.

How I lie in her hand
and her head turns
its circle, over the day
in my head.

Tonight after midnight
my mother and the gesture
I make with my last
cigarette her gesture,
how I wd help her upstairs

when she got drunk on holidays

in terror help her

and always she'd ask for the
last cigarette and fall asleep
with it and I wd handle
the details,

two pillows, window open, and the door
a crack so we could hear
her if she fell out
of bed.

And she did and another cigarette
with her gray hair knotted on the pillow
when I lit it

A poem for record players

The scene changes

Five hours later and
I come into a room
where a clock ticks.
I find a pillow to
muffle the sounds I make.
I am engaged in taking away
from God his sound.

The pigeons somewhere
above me, the cough a
man makes down the hall,
the flap of wings
below me, the squeak
of sparrows in the alley.
The scratches I itch
on my scalp, a landing
of birds under the bay
window out my window.

Details
but which are here and

I hear and shall never
give up again, shall carry
with me over the streets
of this seacoast city,
forever,
        oh clack your
metal wings, god, you are
mine now in the morning.
I have you by the ears
in the exhaust pipes of a
thousand cars, gunning
their motors turning over
        all over town.

6.15.58

A poem for tea heads

I sit in Lees.   At 11:40 PM with
Jimmy the pusher. He teaches me
Ju Ju.

      Hot on the table before us
shrimp foo yong, rice and mushroom
chow yuke.

      Up the street under the wheels
of a strange car is his stash—The ritual.
We make it.   And have made it.
For months now together after midnight.
Soon I know the fuzz will inter-
rupt will arrest Jimmy and
I shall be placed on probation.

                    The poem
does not lie to us. We lie under its
law, alive in the glamour of this hour
able to enter into the sacred places
of his dark people, who carry secrets
glassed in their eyes and hide words
      under the roofs of their mouth.

6.16.58

A poem for painters

Our age bereft of nobility
How can our faces show it?
I look for love.
My lips stand out
dry and cracked with want
of it.
Oh it is well.

Again we go driven by forces
we have no control over. Only
in the poem
comes an image—that we rule
the line by the pen
in the painter's hand one foot
away from me.

Drawing the face
and its torture.
That is why no one dares tackle it.
Held as they are in the hands
of forces
they cannot understand.
That despair

is on my face and shall show
in the fine lines of any man.

I held love once in the palm of my hand.
            See the lines there.
                    How we played
its game, are playing now
in the bounds of white and heartless fields.
            Fall down on my head,
love, drench my flesh in the streams
                    of fine sprays. Like
                        French perfume
        so that I light up as
                    morning glorys and
I am showered by the scent
        of the finished line.

                    No circles
but that two parallels do cross
            And carry our souls and
bodies together as the planets
            Showing light on the surface
                    of our skin, knowing
            that so much flows through
                    the veins underneath.
The cheeks puffed with it.
        Our pockets full.

2

Pushed on by the incompletion
　　　of what goes before me
I hesitate before this paper
　　　scratching for the right words.
Paul Klee scratched for seven years
　　　on smoked glass to develop
　　　his line, LaVigne says: Look
at his face!　he who has spent
　　　all night drawing mine.

The sun
also rises on the rooftops
　　　beginning with violet.
I begin in blue knowing what's cool.

3

My middle name is Joseph and I
walk beside an ass on the way to
what Bethlehem, where a new babe is born.
　　　Not the second hand of Yeats but
first prints on a cloudy windowpane.

4

America, you boil over

The cauldron scalds.
Flesh is scarred.
Eyes shot.

The street aswarm with
vipers and heavy armed bandits.
There are bandages on the wounds
but blood flows unabated.
                              Oh stop
                    up the drains.
            We are run over.

5

Let us stay with what we know.
That love is my strength, that
I am overpowered by it:
                              Desire
                                   that too
is on the face: gone stale.
When green was the bed my love
and I laid down upon.
Such it is, heart's complaint,
You hear upon a day in June.
And I see no end in view

when summer goes, as it will,
upon the roads, like singing
companions across the land.

South of Mission, Seattle,
over the Sierra Mountains,
the Middle West and Michigan,
moving east again, easy
coming into Chicago and
the cattle country, calling
to each other over canyons,
careful not to be caught
at night, they are still out,
the destroyers, and down
into the South, familiar land,
lush places, blue mountains
of Carolina, into Black Mountain
and you can sleep out, or
straight across into states

I cannot think of their names
this nation is so large, like
our hands, our love it lives
with no lover, looking only
for the beloved, back home
into the heart, New York,
New England, Vermont, green
mountains and Massachusetts
my city, Boston and the sea
again to smell what this calm

ocean cannot tell us. The seasons.
Only the heart remembers
and records in the words

6

At last. I come to the last defense.

My poems contain no
wilde beestes, no
lady of the lake, music
of the spheres, or organ chants.

Only the score of a man's
struggle to stay with
what is his own, what
lies within him to do.

Without which is nothing.
And I come to this
knowing the waste,
leaving the rest up to love
and its twisted faces,
my hands claw out at
only to draw back from the
blood already running there.

6.18.58

A poem for early risers

I'm infused with the day
even tho the day may destroy me.
I'm out in it.
Placating it. Saving myself
from the demons
who sit in blue
coats, carping
at us across the
table. Oh they
go out the doors,
I am done with them.
I am done with faces
I have seen before.

For me now the new:
the unturned tricks
of the trade. The place
of the heart where man
is afraid to go.

It is not doors. It is
the ground of my soul
where dinosaurs left

their marks. Their tracks
are upon me. They
walk flatfooted.
Leave heavy heels
and turn sour the green
fields where I eat with
ease. It is good to
throw them up. Good
to have my stomach growl.
After all, I am possessed
by wild animals and
long haired men and
women who gallop
breaking over my beloved
places. Oh put down
thy vanity man the
old man told us under
the tent. You are over-
run with ants.

2

Man lines up for his
breakfast in the dawn
unaware of the jungle
he has left behind
in his sleep. Where
the fields flourished

with cacti, cauliflower,
all the uneatable foods,
where the morning man
perishes, if he remembered.

3

And yet, we must remember.
The old forest, the wild
screams in the backyard
or the cries in the bedroom.
It is ours to nourish.
The nature to nurture.
Dark places where the
woman holds, hands
us, herself handles an
orange ball. Throwing it
up for spring. Like
the clot my grandfather
vomited/months before he
died of cancer. And
spoke of later in terror.

6.20.58

A poem for cock suckers

Well we can go
in the queer bars w/
our long hair reaching
down to the ground and
we can sing our songs
of love like the black mama
on the juke box after all
what have we got left.

On our right the fairies
giggle in their lacquered
voices & blow
smoke in your eyes let them
it's a nigger's world
and we retain strength.
The gifts do not desert us,
the fountains do not dry,
there are mountains
swelling for spring to cascade.

It is all here between
the powdered legs & painted
eyes of the fairy

Friends who do not fail us
Mary in our hour of
   despair. Take not
away from me the small fires
I burn in the memory of love.

6.20.58

A poem for the old man

God love you
  Dana my lover
lost in the horde
on this Friday night
500 men are moving up
& down from the bath
room to the bar
Remove this desire
from the man I love.
Who has opened
  the savagery
of the sea to me.

See to it that
his wants are filled
on California Street
Bestow on him lar–
gesse that allows him
peace in his loins.

Leave him not
to the moths.

Make him out a lion
so that all who see him
hero worship his
thick chest as I did
moving my mouth
over his back bringing
our hearts to heights
I never hike over
   anymore.

Let blond hair
burn on the back of his
neck, let no ache
screw his face
up in pain, his soul
   is so hooked.

Not heroin
Rather fix these
hundred men as his
lovers & lift him
with the enormous bale
of their desire.

Strip from him
hunger and the hungry
ones who eat in the night.
The needy & the new

found ones who would weight him down.
Weight him w/ pride and
pushing the love I put
   in his eyes.

Overflow the 500 with it
Strike them dumb,
on their knees, let them
bow down before it,
this dumb human
who has become
   my beloved
who picked me up
at 18 & put love
so that my pockets
will never be empty,
cherished as they are
against the inside flesh
   of his leg.

I occupy that space
as the boys around me
choke out desire and
drive us both back
home in the hands
   of strangers

6.20.58

A poem for museum goers

I walk down a long
passageway with a
red door waiting for me.
It is Edvard Munch.

Turn right turn
right. And I see
                sister
hanging on the wall,
heavy breasts and hair

Tied to a tree in the garden
with the full moon
are the ladies of the street.
Whipped for whoring.
Their long hair binds them,

They have lain long
hours in bed, blood
on their mouths, arms
reaching down for
ground not given them.

They are enveloped
in pain.   Bah.
There is none. Munch
knew it. Put the
Shreik in their ears
to remove it from his own.

Open thy mouth, tell us
the landscape you have
escaped from, Fishing
boats are in the bay, no
outgoing tides for you
who he anchored to
                    Hell.

Even here the young lovers
cast black shadows.
The nets are down.
Huge seasnakes
squirm on shore
taking away even
the beach from us.
Move on. Moonlight

I see the garden women
in their gravy days
when hair hung golden or
black to the

floor & the walls
were velvet.

An old sailor his face like wood
his chin splintered
by many shipwrecks
keeps their story
in his eyes. How the house
at the top of the drive
held them all, and their lovers,
with Munch the most
obsessed. His face
carved by knife blades.

Lover leaves lover,
1896, 62 years
later, the men
sit, paws and
jagged depths
under their heads,

Now the season of
the furnished room. Gone
the Grecian walls & the
cypress trees,
plain planks and spider
webs, a bed
only big enough for one,

it looks like a
casket. Death
death on every
wall, guillotined
and streaming in
flames.

6.21.58

A poem for the insane

The 2nd afternoon I come
back to the women of Munch.
Models with god over

their shoulders, vampires,
the heads are down and
blood is the water-
color they use to turn on.
The story is not done.
There is one wall
left to walk. Yeah

Afterwards—Nathan
gone, big Eric busted,
Swanson down. It is
right, the Melancholy
on the Beach. I do not
                    split

I hold on to the demon
tree, while shadows drift
around me. Until at last
there is only left the
Death Chamber. Family Reunion
in it. Rocking chairs and

who is the young man
who sneaks out thru
the black curtain, away
from the bad bed.

Yeah stand now
on the new road, with the
huge mountain on your
right out of the mist

the bridge before me,
the woman waiting
with no mouth, waiting
for me to kiss it on.
I will. I will walk with
my eyes up on you for
ever.   We step into
the Kiss, 1897.
The light streams.

Melancholy carries
a red sky and our dreams
are blue boats
no one can bust or
blow out to sea.
We ride them
and Tingel-Tangel
in the afternoon.

A poem for the dead I know

Gather the voices, forces I have forgotten

to find those graves I forget how

to come back to
DAVID ASPELIN
died at 16
put a rifle in his mouth, and laid across his bed at night.
After he held my hand on the way home and said
I will be dead tomorrow.

I see his grave and its pink quartz stone.

And my uncle JOHN
LAFFAN, who I am named after, told me on Christmas
I wont be here next year
and died last week 13 years to the day after his mother
May 13th.
And the blue eyed girl across
the room from me will die. He came home my uncle John
to die in my mother's house, as her mother did
in the same bed, I see her

& RICHARD TWARDZIK, over-dosed in Paris.

I mourn none of them.

I want no one to return, boys & girls who I have known, none
                    to come back,   deck the Coit Tower in American flags,
                    pin flowers in the market windows, we are wrapped
                              in the gloves of God.

Gone for good

the living and the dead, David and John
down, and what about the ones who walk above the ground
                    where are they? where are my lovers?
turned to dust, settling down on barstools.

They sift through the streets of San Francisco.

I feel their hands, I know his mouth as my own.
I want him as I want my own body or me.

                    Her legs to warm my waist.

                    They walk through other rooms,

their desire wails on the face of the full moon,
their pricks rise and make flowers, their hands
masturbate in May rain, and leave me marching

dead arms around my back and stupid tears down
the flesh of my dying face.

I hear their voices on the radio.

II

I now sit 4 flights above Fillmore Street.

The dead are far away.

Underground.

Only the staggering woman in a red coat
Rises. We are all Lazarus
And carry our dead friends with us.

Come up.

Above the telephone wires (if I fell on them
I would have a home tonight.
I would know where I'm going

as the houses fill the hills
as the negro up the steps of 2325

as the birds their blue fields . . .

Green trees, green trees give off the love of my old man.
Neon lights give up the color of a Boston dawn.

There is no death they tell me.
I am on the roof who does not dare to find them out.

III

Dead, be done with them.

How many have I known? Have I counted
as my own. Oh does your flesh sit
on your bones, after these hundred years?

Love, be gone with it.

How many heads have I had under mine?
Strange mattresses for our mistakes.
Does it matter?   The quick mating,
The meeting in public gardens.

Moon, be new to night.

How many things opened at my hands
Are your hands   still   under ground.

Grass, be green on their sunken graves.

A poem for movie goers

I sit in the late evening
    in a quiet restaurant on
    the International Settlement of San Francisco.
My friends, the poets are gone.

Talk of opium and 4 days on horse
    riding across country. Talk of cancer
      sickness sweeping the world
As we, the poets sit. We who should be out
    on battlefields in silver suits
      drink our energies away. David
      talks of hanging wires with no connections.
    And I say we are the conductors.
No wonder Walt Whitman loved them

2

    The records change.
      Green vines hang
down one white column on the balustrade.
There is a marble terrace at my right
and my lover walks miles away.

On the other side of town
where the cable car goes down
and the neon lights stay on all night.

Orange lamps along the wall
and oak leaves sprout too small
My lover's thoughts are not
                    of me at all.

A poem for benzedrine

Voices of the underworld rise stoned to bring me down.
The Law of the land falls on all heads in town.
Declare war the morning is blood red
with reason war is when one of us
dead is worth more than all of Congress
Declare it   I hear it.

Stretched by a window over Polk and Sutter
Sutter another painter stretched by death on his shoulder
sits on his canvas cancer
A country rancid
buries its eyes
with war won over by death
at each instant of life
even our heads the law, half in love with it
in debt to it, we are led by it.
I pay dues in drugs, and keep my pockets full
Out of the mouths of strangers, the sound of friends.
Sue Rosen I heard tonight talking in a Spanish girl.
Demons possess all of America's middle aged women
With houses full of men who whisper and cannot hear
How far out they register the transactions of their souls
I see the studs of Africa passed off as toys

Golden and clay
the feet of lovers walk away.
The sky shoots 15 colors all cool.
The head of God laid in my arms
A junkman who makes it after midnight
Then home to turn on sight laid in his eyes
And ears cleaned out forever by the sound of a motormen's bell
that announces each opening of these doors to Hell.

July 22

She has brought her treasures out into the sun and I spring
to write them down.

4 stills of Charlie Chaplin, "2 by 2" walking on the road
then THE END,

spread out in a circle on

top of the table, ½ an orange rind, the top

of a crystal water jar, a sugar tin, driftwood, green stones
thrushes, my head is still heavy with sleep, the brain cells
not open from the dream.

Of night and the junkies

stealing my bicycle and books. I love them because they are the
boys of my childhood who would chase me home

from school and leave this same terror.

So that even here by the sea,

the objects of my life return, from another life that never dies.

Fish bones, a pin

She brings me in
another tin

charcoal burnt newspaper.

                                        I tell her

                              my dream, how they stole
the bike and I think some clothes because they gave us cigarette
papers to redeem them. Red Sharpe's car and when I got my
clothes back they had someone else's name sewn on the label.
An old name I will not reveal,

                              as I do
the contents of table. The black circle drawn around the hole
in the center, the clinking of pewter as she moves the objects
around, the wash of the waves under us.

July 25

O God of the dawn
   birds protect me
            from the dangers of this world
as I sit in the dark with the crab
   as my ashtray.

   Dreams reveal
         how much in danger we are,
but across the room in the new blue light
       a little girl sits up, her eyes
         wide open staring at me, and
I know it is your sign.
        No matter what disease gets caught
           in my throat.

The waves wash in on the shore and
I find my solace there.
       Comfort against the coming
         of the storm,
        The trial
   arranged by our betrayers.

On H

running the most beautiful blue water

in the sink

vomiting strawberry and green.

July 27

Wrapped up in an Indian blanket
with the mist falling on this paper
I could see miles out on the Pacific Ocean
but fog blocks up the view.

Willa Cather's book
rat eaten rain ruined
beside me, found in Stone House
on a mountain in California.
Book of the prairies, book of love
poems to Spanish Johnny (what rush when I wrote
        his name

on a silver cup bought in Venice
life is sweet together, birds in the branches,
      broken lines
writing them under a roof that opens
     to the sky,
Woman of the prairies writing
        on stone.
Waiting.

Locked out of the world, above a blanket of mist
pierced here and there by notes from a bird,

we are above the sea
   so high the sun
blinds our eyes and the birds
   rise to us,
wheat whirls in the wind.

Read   Vachel Lindsay: *The Golden Whales of California*
        Willa Cather: *April Twilights*

What can I write about
to set my heart afire
as the wood cut and burning
in the stone place on my left.
Here are no demons, only friends.
Does the poem proceed out of pain
does the heart have to beat at a super
and unnatural speed for the word
        to be produced, like the gold
        of alchemy,
transmuted.
        There are no dreams
I have not lived except for

Out the window West and
        the set sun.
In the window a kerosene lamp
        whose light I write by.

To my left the fire in the stone place
            and 4 people before it,
the woman, her daughter and 2 men,
sit on the stone floor, talking of sun
worship and fire worship,
                  the cricket
            in the roof where the bats live,
Still shows a lighter blue than the black
            corners of this room,
                  stone house with wooden
                  doors
on the side of a ridge that rises behind
            the house to a hill

Out the West Window

Out the window West and
      the set sun.
In the window an oil lamp

July 28

A cricket sings in the morning

What to do with the definite article. And
prepositions. How to
connect
without them. I want language to be taut
as the rope
that hold a teapot over
the fire
for hot water.
We pour it. Into the strainer
thru sweet leaves

"The living spirit grows and even outgrows its earlier forms of expression; it freely chooses the men in whom it lives and who proclaim it. This living spirit is eternally renewed and pursues its goal in manifold and inconceivable ways throughout the history of mankind. Measured against it, the names and forms which men have given it mean little enough; they are only the changing leaves and blossoms on the stem of the eternal tree." Jung, *Modern Man in Search of a Soul*, p. 244

This is a stone house built on a ridge in the Big Sur mountains of Southern California. If it were not for the mist which has surrounded us since we arrived, blocking out the sun but not its glare, we could see miles out on the Pacific Ocean. There is a garden built on ridges behind the house. The animals have eaten all the plants. I found two sunflowers at the edge of an abyss, one of which I propped up with pink scarf and stick. They face southwest, giant servants to the sun. We stay in doors all day, the mist being a bright gray glare that is like a wall around and below us.

The house was built in 1919 by a man named Lapler. It is in good condition except for the roof which has been used over the years for firewood. We live primitive on a stone floor, mattresses over wood slabs which give an excellent night's sleep. It is an hour's climb from the road, so all supplies have to be brought in on one's back. There is a large stone fireplace to the right of the doorway which opens West. To the East the kitchen and back-door. All doors are wood. All else is stone. Finely built and of careful craftsmanship. Except of course cabinets and table and stools, which are hand-made from the woods which slope off from this ridge on three sides.

I have trouble with Mass Media

July 29 .

Even my piss runs golden
in this time of plenty
all spring long one lovely
  flowering of my life, and
now in summer I come to
  this mountain, this morning
while below the mist rages. I range
  here clear in the secrets of
    my own being.

Let the peaks be blocked from view
the woman walks thru the room and
brother and sister sit together on the step
    of this stone house.

Lizard under the stone,
bees buzz around us
    in the morning
the two trees full of *canaries* and
    in the burnt grass
        yellow poppies.

the air is alive with sound

Aug 11

A poem for Susan

Just the joy of her
to hear her move in the room,

there is no need to recount actions
description not enough, is like
                    adjectives
but she breathes
                    like a verb, folding
clothes against her belly, brushing
the arms of her coat.

                    Not a cat
                    but woman.
Hidden secret from me before
I watch them unravel their world,

                    bending before the
                    beloved objects in them.

The poem demands a degree of attention that drugs, because they slacken one, deter one from the poem. At least I feel not at my maximum powers. Although a breadth, a dimension is given one that is almost, or not, but irresistible. Each action, object takes on a special meaning it did not have before.

A woman's face.

Both sides of my nature come to the fore with such strength.

The birds, first ones outside my window. The girl fishing in her purse, opening suitcases, and all this at dawn. A magic one I was born at this hour. And we share again the glow and first excitement of that movement, again here. Behind dope. The warmth of mother's womb, with all the hideous knowledge of the world thrown in our face, get wailing behind it.

Because it is the rush

of

life?

September 6

And so Crystal and the man burst into the room on Sunday afternoon about two and started talking about screws. He opened the bureau drawer and answered her questions. For the real dope fiend there is nothing to do absolutely but the ritual of transmuting his dope into his blood and thereby his brain and then noting whatever lies around him, what comes into his ken, Darien, on a peak over the Pacific. He does not look for anything to do, contrary to most people, whatever he does is enough and right. The habit justifies anything. For the habit is a means into the heavenly kingdom. I have not tasted damnation yet. Nor will I. For once there it is eternal. And I dwell forever in higher pastures. Beware poet before you go poking about in the ashes of my life, making ruins out of castles. Castles of marijuana, facades of junk, heroin stairwells, benzedrine flushes, beware before putting a label on any of my garments, my kingdom for a horse. My horse for a cart and I ride back to the Middle Ages, pre-Renaissance man Ezra Pound. I come before the castle.

King Solomon's Magnetic Quiz

FOR R C

And when I went to the woods
    I heard the whispering of lovers
        ages ago. Was it
lights or my eyes playing tricks on me? The trees
were forms, was rain dropping on the ground like feet, was
    fog mist and my old game at hand.
        On my back I heard

    stars creeping up the hill and thought of sex in the dark,
catching him surprised coming around some corner, cradling
    his cock in his hands. Hard it was

        on me to lay there
with only the ground under me. Bits of it stuck
        to my coat. Let it go
    I think; Rise up from this waste. There is no lover
        in the dark. No nightmare stallion
turning into a tree to see
    you; are alone. I rose and went out
        by the secret bush I came in.

'Peyote' poem

With no fresh air in my lungs
                 in the middle of
the night, inhabited by strange gods
                        who
are they, they walk by in white trenchcoats
    with pkgs. of paradise in their pockets.

         Their hands.

Act #2

FOR MARLENE DIETRICH

I took love home with me,
we fixed in the night and
sank into a stinging flash.

¼ grain of love
      we had,
2 men on a cot, a silk
cover and a green cloth
over the lamp.
      The music was just right.
I blew him like a symphony,
   it floated and
         he took me
down the street and
         left me here.
3 AM. No sign.

   only a moving van
   up Van Ness Avenue.

Foster's was never like this.

I'll walk home, up the
　　　same hills we
　　　　came down.
He'll never come back,
　　　there'll be no horse
　　　　tomorrow nor pot
tonight to smoke till dawn.

He's gone and taken
my morphine with him
Oh Johnny. Women in
　　　the night moan yr. name

6.19.59

A Poem for Trapped Things

This morning with a blue flame burning
this thing wings its way in.
Wind shakes the edges of its yellow being.
Gasping for breath.
Living for the instant.
Climbing up the black border of the window.
Why do you want out.
I sit in pain.
A red robe amid debris.
You bend and climb, extending antennae.

I know the butterfly is my soul
grown weak from battle.

A Giant fan on the back of
                    a beetle.
A caterpillar chrysalis that seeks
a new home apart from this room.

And will disappear from sight
at the pulling of invisible strings.
Yet so tenuous, so fine
    this thing is, I am

sitting on the hard bed, we could
vanish from sight like the puff
off an invisible cigarette.
Furred chest, ragged silk under
wings beating against the glass

no one will open.

The blue diamonds on your back
are too beautiful to do
away with.
I watch you
all morning
long.
With my hand over my mouth.

The Acts of Youth

And with great fear I inhabit the middle of the night
What wrecks of the mind await me, what drugs
to dull the senses, what little I have left,
what more can be taken away?

The fear of travelling, of the future without hope
or buoy. I must get away from this place and see
that there is no fear without me: that it is within
unless it be some sudden act or calamity

to land me in the hospital, a total wreck, without
memory again; or worse still, behind bars. If
I could just get out of the country. Some place
where one can eat the lotus in peace.

For in this country it is terror, poverty awaits; or
am I a marked man, my life to be a lesson
or experience to those young who would trod
the same path, without God

unless he be one of justice, to wreak vengeance
on the acts committed while young under un–
due influence or circumstance. Oh I have
always seen my life as drama, patterned

after those who met with disaster or doom.
Is my mind being taken away me.
I have been over the abyss before. What
is that ringing in my ears that tells me

all is nigh, is naught but the roaring of the winter wind.
Woe to those homeless who are out on this night.
Woe to those crimes committed from which we
can walk away unharmed.

So I turn on the light
And smoke rings rise in the air.
Do not think of the future; there is none.
But the formula all great art is made of.

Pain and suffering. Give me the strength
to bear it, to enter those places where the
great animals are caged. And we can live
at peace by their side. A bride to the burden

that no god imposes but knows we have the means
to sustain its force unto the end of our days.
For that it is what we are made for; for that
we are created. Until the dark hours are done.

And we rise again in the dawn.
Infinite particles of the divine sun, now
worshipped in the pitches of the night.

An Anniversary of Death

He too must with me wash his body, though
at far distant time and over endless space
take the cloth unto his loins and on his face
engage in the self same rising as I do now.

A cigarette lit upon his lips; would they were mine
and by this present moon swear his allegiance.
If he ever looks up, see the clouds and breeches
in the sky, and by the stars, lend his eyes shine.

What do I care for miles? or rows of friends lined
up in groups? blue songs, the light's bright glare.
Once he was there, now he is not; I search the empty air
the candle feeds upon, and my eyes, my heart's gone blind

to love and all he was capable of, the sweet patience
when he put his lips to places I cannot name
because they are not now the same
sun shines and larks break forth from winter branches.

My Mother

talking to strange men on the subway,

doesn't see me when she gets on,

    at Washington Street
but I hide in a booth at the side

    and watch her worried, strained face—
the few years she has got left.
    Until at South Station

    I lean over and say:
I've been watching you since you got on.
    She says in an artificial
      voice: Oh, for Heaven's sake!

    as if heaven cared.

But I love her in the underground
    and her gray coat and hair
sitting there, one man over from me
    talking together between the wire grates of a cage.

Cocaine

For I have seen love
and his face is choice Heart of Hearts,
a flesh of pure fire, fusing from the center
where all Motion are one.

And I have known
despair that the Face has ceased to stare
at me with the Rose of the world
but lies furled

in an artificial paradise it is Hell to get into.
If I knew you were there
I would fall upon my knees and plead to God
to deliver you in my arms once again.

But it is senseless to try.
One can only take means to reduce misery,
confuse the sensations so that this Face,
what aches in the heart and makes each new

start less close to the source of desire,
fade from the flesh that fires the night,
with dreams and infinite longing.

6.8

And if to die is to move
from the ugliness of this world
then let it be; should I
welcome spring; turn summer down, and fall

from my hands; the serpent's slow unwinding,
agate eyes, and blue bushes now
in flower; spice smells undo the lament
of tree leaves on the cement.

But if this cannot be
then let it die with the singing
of one lone bird, at twilight
crook the hand, crawl over, cover us with leaves.

Ancient blue star!

seen out the car
window.
One blinking light
how many miles away
stirs in mind
a human condition

When paved alone
created of lust
we wrestle with stone
for answer to dust.

Sickness

I know now heard speak in the night
voices of dead loves past,

whispered instructions over electric air
confined or chained.

Down deep the path's final entrance reveals itself
in will drawn strong on palm of hand.

Do not tamper with the message there.

Do not let silent, secret reaches of the heart
                    invade you here
kept at bay long enough but he is
gone who would protect you from them.

I thought I heard voices in the courtyard
Speaking out
But it was nothing, only wind

Rattling
In a backroom of the city
under an electric light
bulb, naked.

Night's angels descend on us, it's
light become accustomed to our eyes.

Cool wind blows in open window,
I am happy being alone.
It seems time going down an eternal staircase
wound up at ease with me.

I want only the mystery of your arms around me.
Dont worry about eating my food.

Single strand of light falling on his bare shoulder
In the closet.

Won't you come and see me again,
please?

The dragon lies on its side.

Sunset

(Lieder eines Fahren den Gesellen)

Already my spirit soars into the west
smoke rising from a cigarette,
already night birds begin to fall—
leaves lie quiet on the trees.

Where are you, my gone—?
At the hour of your death—and you did die
as surely a bud falls from its stem—
you were scraped from the womb of your mother

        who laughs now and dances in the canyons
                    of New York—

an ant came and deposited the body of its dead brother
                on my pillow,

and the very woods in voices of aunt Ella
            whispered, Hurt
             yourself,
   hurt yourself in the wind,
              at three o'clock in the afternoon
on July 5th

2

May 15th—16 days—May 31
   30 days has September and June
                    makes 46
                    plus 5 in July
  51 days old.   The life of a sparrow.
    Edith Piaf.
                        I would have named you Peter
and that day a boy came to make love to me

          and his name was Peter

An organism, Olson calls the universe.

  "How else can we explain the things that happen to us?"

   Yet does it know
     when one inch is cut off—
                        that this blood boils in my head,
    without wine.

And your name is death to me now,
         vindictive woman
            Magyar—
                  east of the Urals
                  your father came

to wreak havoc on Europe.   Ugrian people
                speaking no language,
                having no poems in your blood.

Only archery, lechery, luxury.

In the Darkness

It's a mistake to assume love
where none exists
we create within our hearts
a worthy object
                    others may share it
and enter that sacred grove but
it is a matter of our caring
                    alone

We want something and
build accordingly but
foolish to believe it
will be there when one needs it the most

                    Alone in a hospital bed
or in jail, I have been
to the Hotel Dixie where no one cared

still within the family breast it lives
and with friends, their parents, of
like recognition of the eyes

I have built a fire now to warm me
through these summer days
I only hope you come back soon
to warm your hands at its dull blaze.

Solitary Pleasure

I wanted a companion, even a lover
to fill the empty mornings, as I knew them
on Columbus and California, but you guarded your
house too well, and the old days were over,
the old nights of jazzing around. You returned to the country alone
with your wife, and children, and I have grieved ever since.

By the seashore, in bed it was worse, days I thought it over
but nights you came back, harder then, whispering under the sheets

I see my hands getting older, and poison smoke playing over the air.
It's only memory of youth I yearn for, what I knew as a boy
the true romance of being loved, waiting for death
that never came, except when one kissed goodbye.

Pressed down by memory, I recollect hours of youth
burning brightly in evening air, how did it go, where
except now I wind up at the Plaza, with no dreams at all.

Pressed flowers fall out of a book, blue and yellow
bound together, it's better than a hotel lobby, or a
lonely tea room, buffeted out of winter snows.

It is the last day of the week, and hard-working shop girls
give thanks the weekend is here, but I have nowhere
to go, no one to see, only the old lantern on the path
to herald someone who never comes back, who has never come here.

Memories of You

Blown the fags in Central Park,
one after another, after midnight
in the snow; on park benches—
under the Japanese Pavilion.

Chased out of Bryant Park,
from behind the monument,
by a cop, with a big black buck.
I fingered his wedding ring
as I blew him. Fled to Boston

and the Esplanade where I was fucked
on the overpass by a student
while hundreds of cars raced by
below, unknowing of our ecstasy?

Returned to Bowery, where I found no one
except one man's hardon
in a doorway, facing the street

Thought of San Francisco, and Union Square,
nothing there and the park on top of Nob Hill,

where I cruised all dawn until finally
a man came out and took me up the backstairs
of the Bachelor's Club and blew me in the bathroom,
I think, locked. In my self? and what use

of this, this purgation of senses. Back to Boston,
jerking off on trains, I gotta stop taking
that wheat germ oil; find a negro at poetry reading
and he fuck me in "skyscraper" over Third Avenue.

Back to trees of Boston and Public Garden,
where I blew men all night long.
The stain is still on my face. How can I
face my brother, who first seduced me—
and my other brother, who I seduced—
and my mother and sister who prays for us all.

Now to Buffalo, where I do nothing—
but jerk off and think of Charles.
Bob Wilson blowing 78 men one weekend
on Fire Island where they serve an Olson martini.

Now back to New York and The Turkish Baths
which I find no fun, tho Frank O'Hara does,
and Allen Ginsberg sits in his white pajamas
and dreams of men as I do—and thinks of fame
at least used to but doesn't have to anymore,
as he is it. And I see what style this has degenerated into,

a vain pulling of my own prick and those of others.
When it was supposed to be a verbal blowjob of a poem.
And I have known women, too, laid beside them in the dawn—
but never balled them. Tho I want to.

Would some woman come up and give me enough of her flesh
so I could ball her and pretend she was a man,
For how else could I do it? For I have a woman's
mind in a man's body, and it would be lesbianism
otherwise, and it is a curse.

Unless some woman see and relieve me of this misery.

2

For I will go to Spoleto and blow them there,
travel back to San Francisco and blow them there,
"get fucked in the ass by saintly motorcyclists"
would it were so; cruise Boston streets again
with Billy Donahue, pretend it is all peaches and cream
while inwardly I scream and dream of the day
when I will be free
to marry
and breed more children
so I can seduce them
and they be seduced by
saintly motorcyclists in the dawn.

Dope

I am old no longer; youth is returned to me
after two sniffs of heroin: The Lift as Char-
les would call it; "have a whiff on me," they
said the old song went in California, as we crossed
the Golden Gate, with Joanne and Nem, Annie

Hatch, etc. Our faces show the strain
at 30. Hah, 30! we'll never see again
why heroin redeems us.

But I dont advise it to the young, or for
anyone but me. My eyes are blue.
                    Are yours too?

                    The rain falls
                    but not on me.

My skin gets a new lift, I dont need no food.
How long will this go on? Only till tomorrow

when I will collapse in a heap on the bed of the world.
Oh destiny, spare me!

Gold-blue jewels of the day. Opalescent rubies
off the moon. Amethyst of the sun. White marbles
at noon,   when the rain falls out
To our ankles. Grey tourmaline, Topaz from Mexico
brought back as booty, a golf ball to adorn
your little finger, can you lift your hand now to fuck the sun?

That's enough. I gotta lie down
                              with memories
                 as my only pillow,
        and rain drops the only thing
                        that's happening,
I wonder what the scene's like in New York.

Baby, I bet it's swinging. In the noon-day, sun.

For Huncke

Knowing no other god than this:
the man who places on your mouth
a kiss. Keep no mystery
but his who whispers memory.

Though he lead you to the desert
or over hills where famine
flowers, like the locust
he devours what he loves most.

Saving none for tomorrow, or dawn
comes with empty arms, and he knows no way
to feed himself, feeding off others,
he has many, who find him, help him

you be one and dedicate your life
and misery to the upkeep of this cheapskate
you love so much no one else
seems to bridge the gap

with their common habits and rude manners,
his never were, a perfect gentleman
who leaves no trace, but lingers through the room
after he has gone, so I would follow

anywhere, over desert or mountain,
it's all the same if he's by my side.
The guide and wizard I would worship and obey,
my guardian teacher, who knows how to stay

alive on practically nothing in the city
until help comes, usually from a stranger or youth.
Such I am or was who knew no better
but all that I better forget now since I met you

and fell into that pit of the past with no escape.
You knock on the door, and off I go with you
into the night with not even a cent in my pockets,
without caring where or when I get back

But if once you put your hand on my shoulders
as David Rattray did last evening
that would be enough, on the seventh night
of the seventh moon, when Herd Boy

meets the Weaving Lady in heaven
and wanders forever lost in arms
until dawn when you come no more.

II Alone

Sustained by poetry, fed anew
by its fires to return from madness,
the void does not beckon as it used to.

Littered with syllables, the road does not loom
as a chasm. The hand of strangers on other
doors does not hurt, the breath of gods

does not desert, but looms large
as a dream, a prairie within our dream,
to which we return, when we need to.

Oh blessed plain, oh pointed chasm.

Stationary

I'm thinking of last evening, the feelings had
lying on the bed, dreaming of boys,

                                 old poets,
Bob Kaufman, seeing him on 8th Street
his hair burning out of his head.
A cigarette smoking in my hand.

A white sweater on corduroy trousers
Hearing voices of fresh lovers on the radio
next door, their spirits rush, you must
remember their kisses their soft murmurings
in the dark, like fundamental things apply
as transient storms return the centaurs.

Berkeley St Bridge

Petrified the wood
wherein we walk.

Frozen the fields.

Cruising these empty city streets
gets you nowhere.

Will you ever be saved, John?
I doubt it.

This world's got nothing for me.

Parking Lot

Don't give nothing for nothing,
yet I blew a guy today
for eight dollars.

He gave me nothing.
I paid him.
O sin that wreaks vengeance

on them lidden children of the world.
I stole the money from Steve Jonas,
'bread from a poet.'

Damned and cursed before all the world
That is what I want to be.

Maine

At last destroyed someone
so many have destroyed me
for a short while what happened
in the trap if accepted

your offer to sleep
or was it that, a confession
of frustration, to become a weapon
against women, their closed womb

temptation to arm myself
at your side against infidelity,
thus bring ourselves the discovery

of endless single beds broken blossom.

We have a flame within us I told Charles
All my old foes turn friends
Why? Because I entered the circle of
the diamond & escaped.
A halo around my head
which burns with the bright glow
of electricity

Impasse

Is it enough my feet blackend
    from streets of the city?
My hands coarsend, lovely bones
    gone to dust.

Is it enough? my heart hardend
arms thickend eyes dim.
Is it enough I lost sight of him
Ages ago and still follow after
    on some blind, dumb path?

Is this aftermath? Am I ever
to follow that, always
The same man, one dream
to death, only another
Dream to never wake from.

Cities stretch eternal streets
lead on. Star-points of light
flicker over the harbor. Oceans
beckon. I cover the waterfront
who have been near no docks.

They are too lonely.
There is no audience watching there
                    through the night
To reflect one's own face
Passing in a glass.

It is eternal audience
and my feet hardend, my heart
blackend, nodding and
bowing before it.

The Old Man:

All about the sexual urge strikes in the night,
lover moves to beloved, mouth closes upon mouth.
Nowhere do the lonely stand long, unattended.
In dark rooms, cocks bulge against trousers.
A dull image, to the sexually uninitiated.

But to me now, come memories of what men call lust,
that excuse which allows them to press up against together moments.

Call it desire. No, more than that. It is need
to possess and be possessed, in oblivion of time.
Know no other cause. Loneliness calls through the house

like a curse, falls on deaf ears. Locked here
blind by poverty, my disease to seek out on dark highway
That lover who will release me into heaven. Dim respite
ends when his arms let go. If even that. No arms
exist for me, but those locked in doors.
In other arms, in love with me, but still sharing
Other arms for ecstasy.

Holy saturday

The Eagle Bar

A lamp lit in the corner
the Chinese girl talks to her lover
At bar, saxophone blares—

blue music, while boy in white turtleneck
    sweater
seduces the polka player from Poland
left over from Union party.

Janet sits beside me,
Barbra Streisand sings on Juke box
James tends bar

It's the same old scene
in Buffalo or Boston
yen goes on, continues in the glare

of night, searching for its lover
oh will we go
where will we search

between potato chips and boys,
for impeccable one—
that impossible lover

who does not come in,
with fresh air and sea
off Lake Erie

but stays home, hidden in the sheets
with his wife and child, alone
ah, the awful ache

as cash register rings
and James the bartender sweeps
bottles off the bar.

There are holy orders in life.
I was born to be a priest
defrocked as Spender says,
on Epiphany to make manifest
                    mysteries.

Bedeviled by women, to cast out their evils
                    and make them whole again.
I am the serpent True, but also god
                    to this devil.

Practicing none, yet part of it.
Oh woe is me, who can create children
                    yet not bear them.
Woe is the woman who comes into my arms.

The Garbos and Dietrichs

Moving like a dream through Ibiza
through midnight cities of the world
buying dreams of men/and their hearts
to hang at dressing tables, how many ornaments
to wear for dinner, or selfish supper parties—

this sin does not show by candlelight, their children
do not hear that cry in the night, odd pregnancies
abortions are not counted, smashed faces
wrenched hearts left behind at harborside
when their ships pull out.

I speak of suicides, men dropped at tide.
I speak of sleeping pills that still our aching mind.
I speak of lovers they murdered because they are so kind.
Anything to stay beautiful and remain blind
To those men they turn into swine.

The blind see only this world
(A Christmas Card

Today the Lamb of God arrives in the mail
above the Cross, beside the Handsome Sailor
                    from Russia
in his turtleneck sweater. Today we make love
                    in our minds.
and women come to fore, winning the field.

It is Christmas, Hanukkah,—heritages we leave
                    behind
        in Israel.

There is a new cross in the wind, and it is our

    minds, imagination, will

    where the discovery is made

of how to pass the night, how to share the gift

of love, our bodies, which is true
                    illumination
        of the present instant.

There is no other journey to make. We receive all
we need.
Without insight, we remain blind.
Without vision, we see only this world.

Loss

To live without the one you love
an empty dream never known
true happiness except as such youth

watching snow at window
listening to old music through morning.
Riding down that deserted street

by evening in a lonely cab
past a blighted theatre
oh god yes, I missed the chance of my life

when I gasped, when I got up and
rushed out the room
away from you.

What Happened?

Better than a closet martinet.
Better than a locket
in a lozenge.
At the market, try and top it
in the Ritz.

Better than a marmoset
at the Grossets,
better than a mussel
in your pockets.
Better than a faucet
for your locker,
better not
clock it.
Better than a sachet
in your cloche,
better than a hatchet
in Massachusetts,
Ponkapog.
Pudget
Sound
lost and found.

Better than an asprin—
                    apertif does it.
Better not ask
                how you caught it
                        what has happened to me?

Better not lack it—
                    or packet in at the Rickenbackers.
                        Better tack it back
                    in a basket
                    for Davy Crockett

        Better not stack it.
            Better stash it
                    on the moon.

                    Oh Pomagranate
                        ah Pawtucket.

                    Oh Winsocki or
                        Naragansett.

            Better not claque it. Better cash it in
            at Hackensack.
                Better not lock it
                    up again.

Suisse

Mountain'd nature is also an enemy
in that it wipes out identity.

Winters are less so
witness my chalet *au vierge*

at least maleficent are more mani-
fest before the hounds of spring

mean nothing, next to it,
the dexterous elements of spring

sound alike, bird; robin, who dunnit?
While winter comes on like a bride,

in night gown, robeing the town.
What about spring, or summer then.

Summer is a communion, don't forget it,
Be a poet to handle it.

The autumn lakes ablaze,
with brown
leaves from summer's ashes. And winter again

Carries autumn out
its lakes gone dry, barren, fertile fields went sour

for what, the dour memory of
wheat fields' gathered harvest.

6.30.69

Sustenance

Your letters and my answer
sleep in a book of poetry;

no often how plenty,
are sure company.

What anacrostic daydreams
disturb this deepest pit

searching at one time for melancholiac act;
fell victims to depression

that cheer me up. They do not stink
no instance how filled with pieties.

Verities of adolescence, proven substance
by companions through childhood,

nightmare's misery
no matter how lost, twisted and illegible

Contorted and painful truth.

Forthcoming

TO FERNAND LÉGER

I died in loneliness
for no one cared for me enough
to become a woman for them
that was not my only thought
and with a woman
she wanted another one

I died in loneliness
of that I am not afraid
but that I am a clank
upon the gutter, a new guard at twilight
without a dream of adolescence
frustration plucked as strong

I died in loneliness
without friends or money
they were taken off
long ago, a melodrama
sounded out my name, the glass key of a
torch song on Father's Day

I died in loneliness
away from the beach and speeding cars

back seat in love with Bunny
on the way to Howard Johnson's
beyond the blue horizon
hunting for a lost popular tune.

6.22.69

Private Estate

         Dancing dandelions
      and buttercups in the grass
remind me of other summer
flowers, simple blossoms

roses and tiger lilies by the wall
         milk pod, sumac branches
lilacs across the road, daisies, blueberries
snaps, cut violets

      three years ago still grow in my mind
as peonies or planted geraniums, bachelor buttons
in downy fields filled with clover
lover, come again and again up fern

path upheld as memory's perennial
against stern hard-faced officers of imprisonment
and cold regulation more painful than lover's arms
or flowers charming but not more lasting.

No, the wild tulip shall outlast the prison wall
no matter what grows within.

6.21.69

Stop Watch

the sensation
1)   of 10 assorted dancers
in a crowded dining room

moving as one person
2)   in unison
to a popular tune

during late afternoon
3)   hip and thighs beat
with sparkling feet

over the stucco floor
4)   before an open door
how fortunate, how poor

we were without the sign,
5)   symbol of recurrence
or occurrence

surrounded
6)   by buff walls
it was not a waltz

only a standard rock
7)   song, much as students
speak in rejoinder

to a classroom; the same decibels
8)   happened in a bookstore when I rose
using the newspaper I had as a fan;

the leaves of clover
9)   fluttering these three
unities I have known

as a tone to a bell's
10)   gong, none of them
lasting longer

than 10–12 seconds
11)   pressing history, light
in memory reckoned.

6.20.69

Supplication

O poetry, visit this house often,
imbue my life with success,
leave me not alone,
give me a wife and home.

Take this curse off
of early death and drugs,
make me a friend among peers,
lend me love, and timeliness.

Return me to the men who teach
and above all, cure the
hurts of wanting the impossible
through this suspended vacuum.

1969

In Public

Promise you wont forget
each time we met
we kept our clothes on
despite obvious intentions
to take them off,
seldom kissed or even slept,
talked to spend desire,
worn exhausted from regret.

Continue our relationship apart
under surveillance, torture, persecuted
confinement's theft; no must or sudden blows
when embodied spirits mingled
despite fall's knock
we rode the great divide
of falsehood, hunger and last year

1968

Billie

He was as a god,
stepped out of eternal dream
along the boardwalk.

He looked at my girl,
a dream to herself and
that was the end of them.

They disappeared beside the sea
at Revere Beach as
I aint seen them since.

If you find anyone
answering their description
please let me know. I need them

to carry the weight of my life
The old gods are gone. What lives on
in my heart

is their flesh
like a wound,
a tomb, a bomb.

1966

Acceptance

Should I wear a shadowed eye,
      grow moustaches
   delineate my chin

accept spit as offering,
      attach a silver earring
   grease my hair

give orders to legions
      of lovers to maintain manhood
   scimitars away as souvenirs?

Sooush, beloved! here is my tongue.

Deprivation

Roses, lilacs and rains
over smell of earth, freshly
turned Saturday morning for
lovers' walks down strange lanes.

Never again recaptured
never again to find, oh how
our mind rebels at this, never
again to kiss that girl

with amethyst eyes, or watch
sunrise over the harbor, never again
to visit the grape arbor of childhood,
or remove the memory stain

of these events from our firm, budding youth,
mad truth of these trysts to lose
in time their hidden passion & meaning.

Indignation

It doesn't matter if one lives or dies
without desire. I tried to go away
on my own. Instead came back home

defeated to more defeat, worse
that it was met by discord
of an hideous sort, cursing and swearing

from a lower class of orders, dying at the doorstep.

All the men I wanted were married to others
and poetry in my heart burned
out. Left at afternoon ill,

what I approached
was to fall dead by my own hand
or close to it, nervous, afraid to move

I cannot blame them, only the men I wanted
are not here anymore, still the possible
freedom of their love is my dream.

1970

The Suck

This morning
last evening, yes
terday afternoon

        in the hall
your voice, full
of complement

turns to strike
someone you do not

know as a wife or brother,

shaking, trembling
in your arms
sweating like seventeen

again under young middle-aged

bellies in the summer.

1968

Reading in Bed

by evening light, at the window, where wind blows
it's not enough to wake with morning
as a child, the insistent urge of habit

sounds, to write a poem, to pore over one's past
recall ultimate orders one has since doubted
in despair. Inner reality returns

of moonlight over water at Gloucester, as
fine a harbor as the Adriatic, Charles said, before the big storm
blew up to land ancient moorings, shards against sand

of memory at midnight; ah yes the dream begins
of lips pressed against yours over waves, tides,
hour-long auto rides into dawn, when time

pounds a mystery on the beach, to no death out of reach.

January 9, 1970

The Travel of Imagination
through Time

a blue brooch
on the bureau,

a white cadillac
in lit yard

as flesh falls
before glass

in surprise, years pass un–
naturally, in object–

ion to calendars.
Time not measure

of man, but what he may do,
with himself, in this hour,

this minute, this instant—
false divisions of the moon,

the sun, mathematics.
Who to know

dark regions eyes see
we measure as ours,

on the street, in the city,
in bed, before time's awake

in the middle of blackness
when one lies alert

after an argument,
he may sense

the cautious breath of a friend,
presumably, also up,

in the dark of his house,
who alike hears your thoughts,

wondering; that is true meeting in eternity.
Not this petty worry

about days, months, proximities
to warmth. There are always fires

on earth, that burn immortally.

Viva

FOR FRANCIS W. SWEENEY, SJ

Drag them out of their places,
for they block the progress of our lives, our times,
drag them out of their graves,
even if they were our parents,
for they barricade the streets of our protest, our loves;

contaminate afternoons with lanterns from poems
by questions of industry and idleness,
to swipe the mystery of storms and floods
through a stare of smug aristocracy.

Even though revolutionary epics have survived
they remain at the bottom gates
holding posts to poison the flows of experiment.

Keep fires down low to protect error, challenging uses
of light and worship, unless it be one
of trite conformity to their texts.
Encourage poverty by their avoidance
of the problems from our weird needs

That they have refused to consider
Except in terms of bare hospitality or prison
Yes, days are long they have judged

Fruitless and rewards sweet they reject
To be worthless. The nights have come that
They retire early; yes drag them out of their places
For they breed death and young graves, heartless despair
Stealing beneath bosoms to fester automatically in leeches
As enormous tumours out from the poverty of their lusts.

Here for the Night

at 7 dollars for a single room's rest, and
  asylum from the city's municipal officers,
often spending the night, wandering over by the river
  in the city's parks and dumps, walking the streets, by-
ways and avenues Romantic-less dawn found me,
                           resting in some bookshop, that
  opens early, or never closes, as it used to, the fresh

pranks, and hi-jinx of the stubborn generosity
                that rests within hearts of men.

    Sunday evening, barely a sound, but the television
  it's the image of a bed that sets off the sexual transgression
           or retreat

's Paul Benzaquin 931-1640 asks, Station 7's announcer anyway
              broadcasts
  reports toward the viewer upon sexual relations, as far as the Y

           the grey windows, rattling maid
           diseased clients broach no new adv.
           for the place today more than they did
           two years ago, or ten when I was in love.

Only those memories sustain me now
outside the girl knocks
to make up my room, while Turbo jets glow
in the sky above Boston docks

I have settled in this town
I shall not play the painted clown

I shall seek the major release
to win the goal of my heart's need

Returning to the mood of a city,
where there resides only a single person, I could call
on, whom would welcome one at this hour, dirty
I return to this paper to write what I shall,

about the hammer above the courtyard, and the insistent
sexual requirements forcing *un pauvre amour* out for decades
to huddle up together in alleys, and dream the ideal structures
Whitman's predictions or prophecies foretold would for the
                              remaining three decades of my life.

The Pool Hall

in an abandoned toilet,

did the lights still work,

the asylum was a barracks, in the next building
that's where they keep them in Front and Center, he could just see
     EC 6 and EC 8, did they flush

the Broadway feelings porch, the desolate tone of derelict hotels,
peeling walls, absent telephone, posted notices no one read,

unremembered trophies, an empty soap dish

  The long, narrow halls, unopened doors
    and striped red and green forlorn streamers from a forgotten festivity

How the wind blew in May, with cracked ledges
past the bars, stone cold, could it be old memory

        was keeping another cold potato to
          rustle up an ancient scene,
        venerable, hearing rain upon eight foot screens?
        and an empty cup for cigarettes,
                of water.

Money Is Not Monogamous

A poor man cannot make use of himself.
He is demoralized through excessive beat exertion.
He cannot take orders even for the good of himself
Usually quite to the contrary.

He surrenders for despair although believes surrounding conditions.
He produces fiery revolution in unconscious rebellion.
He believes anything that happens
as misfortune of others.

Quickening as rain on highways, he plunges into chance
faith, duty or conscience culminating legends
of eros, beauty, will & condition
upon distance or parent organization.

He swims with the tide, taking care
he has undressed for it & surveyed its relation
to majority use, freely contributing to its content & current form,
little saving resources toward relentless tides

of time, shallow depths & eventual discharge.
He recognizes none of these fears, not their predicted fact.

The Loneliness

It is so sad
It is so lonely
I felt younger after doing him,
and when I looked in the mirror
my hair was rumpled.

I smoothed it
and rooted for someone else
or wanted to satisfy myself,
Almost seven,
No hope left.

How can a man have pride
without a wife.

I spit him out on the floor.
Immensely relieved
After ejaculating
Imagining myself up my lover's ass
he coming by himself.

Looking out the window, for no reason
except to soothe myself

I shall go to the bookstore
And pretend nothing happened.
Enormously gratified.

Feeling like a girl
stinking beneath my clothes.

Sexual facts are tiring, too

Ignorance, seduction
There is a certain titillation / that surrounds the air, / where you live
The movement of hips past the car window
The relentless search for release

in cabaret, on the riverbank

The group of homosexuals invades the city.
They are decimated by time, alcohol

and each is left with his own condition

The green scarf from the cabinet door
provokes self-extension.

Ascertain stimulation from living in the city,
seeing the beautiful women,
hearing the drums start in the early afternoon

I Hope It Goes On

A blinding rain storm behind The Beacon Chambers
       and out in front denizens scatter under
    inclement thunder. Joanne Kyger

moseys down to Brooklyn before Bolinas, this hymn
          shall honor her devotion over 15 years
       to maidenhood blessed by poems.

It's not enough to compare her
       to movie stars, Jane Fonda or Broadway intellectuals
          Breaking shower lighting in Max's Kansas City

And as sudden as it started, this downpour ends. Class
       that's what she got, what gives you a thrill
          listening to her in Bob Creeley's living room

read or dancing out in Berkeley, 1965 after returning from Kyoto.
        Columbus Ave hoyden days, tripping down Telegraph Hill
       I remember her at Halfway House managing

time-spheres as deftly as orange plants or egg-plant salads.
     In New York, heroic against warehouse derelicts and
       dressing out in middle-class fur coats, for a day on the town.

It's not enough to be simply beautiful, one must manifest
magnificent sex and brains,
besides, endurance and in the sunlight, by the windows at Annisquam

Music

FOR GERRIT

What is poetry? an image
    in the mirror;
reflection from a broadside
  pinned to the wall,
  penned by a friend,
    from where old feelings
    old meanings arise;
relief from pain; the diligence of work.

Mysterious words upon a page in adolescence;
listening to poets read. What is poetry?
    Breath, competence, success
or simply Eros.
        "Four sides to every thing."

The increase in electricity causes lights to flow.
  Is it only light, or heat,
    words ordered in a row.
Men or gods. I'll never know
    or try to know
      more than the doing,
        the flowing
rain upon the roof. That one hears,
      and reveres

inside, away from the cold
within the house
where the heat

reminds one of what it is to be like
out in the cold
rushing over the field
mad,

Intelligence or emotion?   language.

Yonnie

1

Beneath the ivory lady
  of mercy
Red wings
upon a silver tray
a gold bracelet laid
there before retiring.

Real love, at last
half-pretending, half Creel-
eys,
    her voice
          as if youth should go on forever
     beneath a blue star.

2

· Listening in the dark
to a piano thirty years old,
it's not as in the old days,
when I got up,

I had to cross the room
to turn on the light

now it's beside the bed,
when I write "ASSEZ."

JOHN WIENERS
BEHIND THE
STATE CAPITOL
OR
CINCINNATI
PIKE

UNDERSTOOD DISBELIEF IN PAGANISM, LIES AND HERESY

Prick any literay dichotomy
sung unrent gibberish from maxim skulls
west Manchester cemetery

recidivist testimony damned
promulgated post-mortem Harry Ghouls
wills pleasant chicanery hulled

in opposition to queer honesty,
flying hapless good humours
Morphe erroneous untedious mystery,

non-said mistakes; pure levity
to a method of confused doubt;
lipping erratic contrary indexd

Brevity; yes or no arsinine Coliseum
arrogance, attrib. Constant shout
Emperor Hippocratic misaligned

green breviary Ursuline stiff codecil.
A prayerbook, black Catholic mint
bogus mendicants Parsifal muff

Taught in the text as poor flopped sisters,
reeked convent blood between pleas
of gospel purblind drawn melodramas.

Silk-ribbon circus twined, border rhyme.
Povertystricken grandfathers hymnal
Less-allowed than San de Remo cape civil

War Reolutionary caval.
House Father across Sunday common roof
"But they're all ivoried brooch (navel

running marines the other way."
Spies vision for impertinently, drugs
when you're awake.

A viscosity submandered elopes
deluge senseless colophon
Forgotten opposition

in the face of negligent monetary
station or bookstore adherent nation.
(Debauched, bequeathed goad.)

DOM PERIGNON

1959

One of us is going to die,
I dont know which
champagne and cake on the balcony
geraniums newly planted after the rain,
dogs baying to the moon.
The geraniums,
their faces freshly painted
flow/in the moon, also of the wall
with a luminous red I have never seen before --
at twilight --
the sky grey
but the geraniums
vibrous
different than the firefly
different than the contralto
singing
Schubert's Last Songs,
four of them
different from the Bavarian Gentians
of Lawrence.
Only you, geraniums alone
of the moon.

Unpublished Composition Dennison Road, Summer Annisquam,

1966

CONTEMPLATION

Why do they turn away from us
on the streets when we love
them. Billie Holiday was the story
of my whole life & still is

on sunlit Sunday afternoons

opposite the elevated railroad
tracks
at Cambridge street & Charles
when every hope burns to stinking incontinence,

the winter wind blows sand & sea off countless holiday
extravaganzas, between body & soul

Sultry California boulevards proliferate upon a shredded
mortality, as the abyss of former promenades wells

to fecundate interiorly
again at Land's
End.

The pleasures of young escapades envelopes
smoked glass store-fronts outside the empty Scotch & soda
orders.
Bar.

HIATUS

Rest in the dream, that's all I can do.
Hear bells tinkle on the grass
and birds sing.

Smoke in bed
wait for your return
all morning long.

Sit on silken pillows
worked with peacock designs
and golden swans.

Write poems
before a yellow table
in the dawn all morning long.

See Mrs. Coyle the landlady
eat milkweed drunkenly
then do three days' dishes
in the sink all morning long.

Watch her pass before the dragon lilies,
lock the foundry shed,
each single event invested with divinity,
then the pause
when no words come
for the rest of the morning.

A NEW BENEFIT

Mints informer
by permanent comparison
unallowed good rebuttal

I'm almost dropped to
my seat, honest

injun.
shoddy interiors dis
avowed

props & opening
nite bouquets

restored

---

rented in New Jersey.

Anecdote

After several years of having her in their midst, the locals find Mrs. Onassis tame news indeed. They are inclined to ignore her, which she likes.

Only one anecdote has ever circulated about the famous renter. It seems the Casey farmhouse has a French fence around it, a fence of narrowly woven stakes.

Jackie telephoned her landlords and said she'd like to take the fence down. She said her husband, who is rather short and stocky, couldn't see over it, and she wanted Ari to be able to enjoy the view of the neighboring town and hills.

The Caseys refused the request, but did send over a workman who cut a panel out of the fence and put it on hinges.

Now, when in residence, the panel can be lifted. And Aristotle Onassis, that wily world traveler and cosmopolite, a Greek born in Turkey with Argentinian citizenship, a man reputed to be worth one thousand million dollars, can sit and admire the view of Peapack, New Jersey!

Around the environs of the Essex Hunt there are some ambivalent ideas expressed about Jackie Onassis which echo the kind of "yes, she is" — "no, she isn't" opinions often heard around international salons.

There are those who admire Jackie's down-to-earth approach to her bucolic weekend life out of Manhattan, her desire for privacy, and her hope to get away from it all and back to nature.

But there are also those who accuse her of always wanting it both ways for herself.

These are the "does she

'Jackie wanted a fence taken down so that Ari could enjoy the view'

FOR WHAT TIME SLAYS

Scheduled *Summer 1962*

The fog flung over the fields.

The dew heavy on the individual stalks of grass
or weed. The beetles making just the right sound
in the woods, and on the top of the highest tree,
a bird cackling.
The smell of green weeds on the pathway. Whitman's
poems to MANHATTAN, "Give me the splendid silent
sun" all the crowds now dead.
And in the day I am tormented by the memory of
warm supper clubs at night, never crowded, the
way a young man opens the door,
        Mambah singing therè, as Mabel Mercer, on a
                kitchen chair.
        For I have looked down into the pit and turned
        away trembling.

C H I L DREN OF THE WORKING CLASS

to Somes

from incarceration, Taunton State Hospital, 1972

gaunt, ugly deformed

broken from the womb, and horribly shriven
at the labor of their forefathers, if you check back

scout around grey before actual time
their sordid brains don't work right,
pinched men emaciated, piling up railroad ties and highway
ditches
blanched women, swollen and crudely numb
ered before the dark of dawn

scuttling by candlelight, one not to touch, that is, a signal panic
thick peasants after *the* attitude

at that time of their century, bleak and centrifugal
they carry about them, tough disciplines of copper Inidanheads.

there are worse, whom you may never see, non-crucial around
the
spoke, these you do, seldom
locked in Taunton State Hospital and other peon work farms
drudge from morning until night, abandoned within destitute
crevices odd clothes
intent on performing some particular task long has been far
removed
there is no hope, they locked-in key's; housed of course

and there fed, poorly
off sooted, plastic dishes, soiled grimy silver knives and forks,
stamped Department of Mental Health spoons
but the unshrinkable duties of any society
produces its ill-kempt, ignorant and sore idiosyncracies.

There has never been a man yet, whom no matter how wise
can explain how a god, so beautiful he can create
the graces of formal gardens, the exquisite twilight sunsets
in splendor of elegant toolsmiths, still can yield the horror of

dwarfs, who cannot stand up straight with crushed skulls,
diseases on their legs and feet unshaven faces and women,
worn humped backs, deformed necks, hare lips, obese arms

34

distended rumps, there is not a flame shoots out could extinguish the torch of any liberty's state infection.

1907, My Mother was born, I am witness t-
o the exasperation of gallant human beings at g-
od, priestly fathers and Her Highness, Holy Mother the Church
persons who felt they were never given a chance, had n-
o luck and were flayed at suffering.

They produced children with phobias, manias and depression,
they cared little for their own metier, and kept watch upon
others, some chance to get ahead

Yes life was hard for them, much more had than for any blo
ated millionaire, who still lives on
their hard-earned monies. I feel I shall
have to be punished for writing this,
that the omniscient god is the rich one,
cared little for looks, less for Art,
still kept weekly films close for the
free dishes and scandal hot. Some how
though got cheated in health and upon
hearth. I am one of them. I am witness
not to Whitman's vision, but instead the
poorhouses, the mad city asylums and re-
lief worklines. Yes, I am witness not to
God's goodness, but his better or less scorn.

The First of May, The Commonwealth of State Massachusetts,
1972.

"*I'm only asking . . . that I shall be shot with him,*" said Claretta Petacci, his mistress.

re Soup Poets   with John
st 12, 19, 26 of culture
e held at the Hatch She

40

THE   HO MECOMING II

for Stephanie Bright

It depends on who they're in love with, where, when, and

why, and for whom?

1957 3 weekends ceaseless
38 Grove rear
3rd 33 South Russell

S T R E E T

a 2nd floor whole
quitted 37 Middlesex November
   c a u s e

C A P T A I N
Jack's June ete guests

Post sloan h   o   u   s   e
Wa s   h   i   n   g   t   o   n   Y
G U T t ed E l i o t   S T R e e t
base   front X 2 M e x i c a n T o t e m

H   a   l l Codexes
hearing Peggy's voice in the men's room — Ronnie's through Tom
Tom's Toil -ets
STeve's "I murraid Huey Newton;" f o r f e i t i n g
CARLotta Stoppato Venetian non-negre'Roi LEvine was born,
George Bra   ziller.

"I died my time in Danvers for nothing; I paid my graduation
present
t ȯ   J a c k y over Humphrey's pa-
t e n t l y   z   e   r   o redeemer.

"Where does their money come from? Rubirosa Capitol
Havana CUBa;
National tabernacle drill compell.

T h e y g e t b a c k, s l e e p 3, t h e res t of
Friday
before 12,   i   n   t   h   e   house,
g o o d as new, honest   over April lost weekend.

I couldn't tell you a thing I've done: what's the difference;
lush
how I'll g e t   home.

As submitted to Poetry in Public Places.

S   E   Q   U   E   L   T
O A P   O   E   M   F OR

PAINTERS

Abutting solidity apart
the   i v y circuit,

real envy at convention-
aon in the living room.

17
Irving Str. even that the
A   R   M   Y
Base, subway car shookdown

past Andrew blew the whistle, lights
on in the downstairs, or were
they doused That new year's lodge

Buck's County birth
day Blizzard? Sis
I can stand new friends

& If I had old ones, damned
to estimate allot-

2
Cavernous echoes obeyed lines no
heartache, only hangover upper

GRANT's Ave. horizon shriners
C
E
ntral Park dawn moonshiners lent,
                              back
stretch small Hoosiers baker scratched
N
i
ckel trays when Mary had a little
arnd. the corner Corp. *Time* when rout went all cost
to s h   i   r   k the cheap blouse, ba-
se-   m   e n t reject. Who I, or the babbling collar?

Government means currency
parenthetically government without currency means government
less subterfuge *ranean.*

S E C O N D S summer celibate cushioned with Eight
T
E
L
E
phones in 3 years
b l a ck, bronze
grn, wall bed, red white etc.
c o f f e e s ill.

The winter winds howl
above the loop amid-November
while
the cherry toneamber Louisianyan beads

c oast severance
                    Dix parity
SAy mid-lunch, papa
pack   up yipⅤp paper never stray or

toast Albi
C H O O S E fla   v   o   r *over*
train, instead, one-quarter rats I1   quart IV-

"Get him out of my head, now they quote
he's a GREat poet, put him back to hbed.
Get rid of him." Home after work, for what
B o a r d; Tele   vision, never cocktails.
Greasy hamburgers I got
cooking, now, you're getting out
of hand
            small, potatoes over
close, call, filly smoke.

Work possibly crow haul back
jaunty tips daily plough petit
Whitcomb Horse-tout endowed em p l o y- ed
Hasaid.

LETTERS

Please excuse handwriting as we are batting along Highway
64 I N T O Memphis

F R O M New York City, I tried to call you 5 or 7 times as I
LEFt my only suit hanging on back of Balas' living room door.
Along with khaki jacket. It is navy blue with thin pinstripe.

Amidst the welter of your days, would it be *too much* for
you to box this & ship c/o Rumaker. I wldn't ask but there is
no one else. As it is I fear it already sold in the hunger of their
days. Tom will remember once you mention it. If you can't
reach him home try Alan RI2-1960. You see if he is evicted the
clothes may get lost. New York is deolate. With non-committ-
ment the virtue. The movies requiring or worth more of a man's
attentions. Thus I missed the intensity of you & me. Also I ran
into the police & narcotics squad and I was followed for one
day and ½ by a force of them until I left the Bigtown. So if
there are questions there from strangers about any of us, be wary.

The story: I spent the dawn
one morning walking up Fifth Avenue window shopping/writing
down addresses of shops I wd. come back to Monday, enroute
from Pennsylvania's 34th Str. Sta. Monday from 4 to 6 AM I
spent in Union Square not noticed the same cabdrivers circling
wherever I seemed to wander. Eighth Street, Sheridan Square,
Washington Square — the same faces. I didn't worry. But early
dawn (having waited a 2hr rainstorm under a newspaper kiosk,
with a young bum asleep on my lap) I looked across and saw
two figures light a pipe in the shadow of The Union Square
Savings Bank. After a while one of them crossed directly over
to me while the other slid down the shadows and disappeared.
The one coming to me, a Kerouac-type ascamper with a pipe in
his mouth. He didn't say anything but walked past me & into
the park. I did not turn around. After a while, I walked
down towards a restaurant, had a cup of coffee, & walked back
in front of the bank, more leftside *de la rue*. It was daylight
now and I kept walking uptown. But changed my mind & *walk-
ed* out into the street heading back where I came from. I saw
this car which had been coming toward me — stop. I walked in
a diagonal, & the car advanced. I went very fast until I came to
a monument, & then turned back quick again catching the car
following me. I ran into the park, the car pulling up in to the
parking space, beside the monument.

Then I realized that I had done nothing but *perhaps* witness
a score, or just attracted some attention by a red sweatshirt I was
wearing, or in my own, near conclusive September High eastate.
Also earlier, after "Kerouac" had gone into the park, a man came

78

up from the subway, where we were dozing (the bum still asleeping) and spent, in this intermittently gusty and rainy twilight 30 minutes me, I thought, for a pick-up, & then after he kept his attentions on The Bank; I said, "I know what time it is," (He had asked me) "I saw it over there," motioning to Bank.

In the Park, a man, as I was hurried by, was executing these frantic set-up exercises, supposedly. Morning sit-ups, Georgian contortionist, Balanchine suspension, consisting of hand-wavings, toe-touches, and when I stopped outside park, he began bouncing on his feet, as tho heralding Hon. Graham Wilson, current Gov. of or from Upstate Albany, N.Y., bending his knees, erstwhile waving his arms in the air.

I decided I would find out what I was in. Whether I was foolish, modish, or famous due to Angna Ford hallFORum Enters. Also I did not want to lead these approaching maturity's crescent men back to Poet Frank and Joseph O'Hara's. For one hour, like a sucker, I played copus superlative robbers up and down NY STS.

Certainly, making them think, my antics as a neo-groupie post Incorp. SOLe PUBlisher of MEASURe, a quarterly that has appeared in 15 years THRICE I was some sort of connection for this score, which either, as I had so oft committed without realizing from The Department of Drugs and Dangerous Substances, they had staked out, in hot pursuit for my corpus, in dubitably, no less my antics brought their attentions to.

They dress as middle-class workmen. Lunchbags, softhats & zippers jackets.

They also all carried newspapers. And would not meet my eyes, which taunted * I dare you. Believe, and they always, did. Innoviaetate, underplayed, deigning mein, and illuminate. One clenched his fists as he turned a corner behind which I was waiting, in fixation affront, semblance *sourire*. I got so tired I took a couple more turns, and solutionless, piqued, head leafily home. Out of my wits, consult. eager colloquy, O'Hara and the then LeSeur went to work. A *chic* duo, in Frnch Livre, l'autre MOMA, assistant *cure*.

(Earlier, partying enacte, intros to youths, Virgil, Morris, even younger Bradley, Bunny, Gregory, John LaTouche, Jimmy, Edwin, Grace *au* telephone.)

The Second Letter composed to ROBin Blaser, employed at Widener Library, resident on Lime Street, near Charles Mall, in part contains suffixes to the pleasure, observed southernly bd. They were never mailed, for months from the *16* months contemplation.

79

America, despite your motels and outhouses, with the picture window, exhilarates me, your fields of sunflowers-daisies. The day's eye falls, we speed Route 66 after it. New York, we leave behind. Its movie-house poets and its Federal men, who follow me on the streets, all the streets, G-men, earnest to pin me down as a detonated cornice behind bars. Take America out of my eye and imprision us all. They have set, like Art Rimbo *for me*, snares and slide through. They popenjai miscreants, misanthrope. Who unwrapped in his hands round boxes to trap me. Or placidly tapped me on my wrist, circling darkly strangely cabins, masonically in Alan's scarlet pullhoft. I got out. Prime race across country. Each straitcut west. The chauffeur is *blonde*, but built as braun for hirsute Werner Engelhard von Braun. You know, I have never felt well, since I grew hair on my ass, calling me by my Ma's nom. The country flat, sounding electronic rubbers. As E.M.G. Remarque, *pour le temps etre*, out-distanced. Vistas open. Jamais, plains peace corps. White cotten balls line the highway, and the sun hardens my skin. My eyes cleaned of soot. America's civic imprimatur. United Kingdom's by-laws. We pass enormity's diesel motors. That flunky with his wounds, scarFace, did not halt his pity. Their spy as Mom unfooled Century prevarication. Tobacconist stalling as caterers eternal returns or dry cleaners' glassily ogling Liggetts' shouldered no detour to Philadelphia. The beau with his suitcase full of stolen goods followed Fat Greenstreet, not I him, up Fifth Avenue, hopping a bus, at 22nd, a girl kept her hands fattygrease, rubbing her knee against chapped deprivation. *Handbag open.* I dropped despite her request no passed transaction of blank cruces. I saw same identities fracture working salvation. My last day East.

By evening Penn Station four thousand re-assembled. Some made quiet obscene noises as I walked by them. One asked where his train for Newark was. Even a 16 year old, they dressed adulterously. A patsy covered the needlehole on his Mainline. His eyes whimpered for my Fixe. I went by. I sang. "I know that you know," but I know you too. Every store I went, they tailed flat foot, gumshoed, especial mortDad, who I read, from a distance, slipped Chas. Pharmaceuticals this note1 *The man you are waiting on is a narcotics suspect. Do nothing to arouse his suspicions, please watch him.*
I wanted to scream in an Eighth *Street* Marboroshop. It got so bad, I thought they were taking *Pictures*, and self-demonstratedly strolled against a book to my face. Recreated as Greta Garbo. Inadequate to laugh anymore, when I passed them on that oft-trailled Rensalleer Gardens gradually vending Avenue of the Americas. Chewing my lips, grinding teeth. They as 'Sciapps' possibly had me. Shifts changing, early 60's later, from Dior to Mu-mus, late 40's reference. New ones the gang, that old cagey Philomena, didn't recognize anymore. I wanted to warm

residuals in *Boston*. For the life of Her, as beatification, I didn't
dare. If I could only make my train out.

        If I loved you less
        should you love me more,
        or if I cared for you
        would you not care for me?

        What foolish question to ask
        two who were in love
        as if answer prove
        what one already knew.

        We do not live, nor shall
        we die whose destinies
        entwine, extant as a star
        caring more for you by far.

Now nothing but this 6 foot highway from Oklahoma City to the
sea. To the ashes of Lawrence. We follow the rivers, we follow
the railroad, follow the sun, their driver says. It is its setting,
speeding on the path, we cannot be entrapped, unto Taos, Sante
Fe, New Mexico. It is open, and apathetically *reductio ad absurd*,
to quotationedly registration, murderous *sine* dubbing: psalter
Maybelline wearisome, in length of receipted Dicky, ho.

The dernier epistle, before coming back to apartmentless et trans-
ferred Professor Blaser, West Cedar, kitty juncture Phillips, top
garrett, even since a LDC served to obtain the garments, was not
deposited before Valentine off Leavenworth, two per four Jets,
schmecter. NOVEMBEr 13, 1957.

      We were stopped in the South. We produced our papers.
We were allowed to pass. We arrived in San Francisco. I was safe.
My packages had been opened on arrival at Rumaker's by the Post
O F F I C E: *Ten* days later, Commonwealth STAte
California the negro, who had tapped my wrist on west broadway's
22nd S t r e e t got on The MIS s i o n B O u n d
T H I R D a n d K e a r n y S T R E E T overland
as I from down T O W N B   a y C I T y A R E A
transferred at Market, to re-enter my borrowed S E C O N D
F L O O R Washington CableCA r train stop. The P U S H
E R H U B   had earlier got in, near C   I T Y
L I G H T C   O L U M B U S, having sd,
Wow, in his ear. He has nodded to me since. He has given me
sp e e c h e s F R E E L O A D I N G, that

81

pressure is off, A T T H E P L A C E, if y ou a re
l o oki ng for S T E A M   H E A T, see him.   It
began   a g a i n.

13 durable paper wrapt cartons of illicitly? gaind volumes were
O P E N E D. A   N   D   S E A R C H E D.
The S L I P C A S E S on The Heritage Club editions
had been sliced with a razor blade, they were too too dumb to
see how, precisely without cognizant, to check.   R U M A
K E R was A R R E S T E D for V A G R A
N C Y around M I D N I G H T on POLk S t r e e t,
in what they lingo-wise shop- T A L K E D The Gulch
sober and six feet away from a nearest man. PHOTO-Graped
and F I N GE R PRINTED.   M O n maitre Maison,
one semi decade *inamorata* was arrested for drunkeness upon
H A Y E S S T R E E T. And they put
raise one space   into
his cell, imprisoned involitionally a negro who recounted he was
arrested for trafficking, inviolationedly for Canadian Aspirin,
ovarian codeine. Attempted gang-craze.
The newly arrived Queen Examiner and Chronicle to our know-
ledge staying with a Fort Wayne, Indiana House Merchant
Painter, declined to print this atrocity. Certifiedly they trans-
cripted others, carrying resemblances in V   E   I N   S,
intimating automobile Screen Silent, Francis X. BUShman and
Violette Verdy, Prima Assolua of City Center Ballet,
francished to Nursing Rt. S H O R T committed
larceninous gunshot mutilations upon sleeping visitors after
nearly two years labor at FRUIT STREET infirmaries,
nearby   b   a   c   k   t   o   i   l. Lights were flashed
on in our windows. Early AM, after came height, knocking on
doors, when alone, Mr. D   U   R   K   E   E   and H O S T
at TOM FIELDS, ROBERT DUNCANS, AND JESS COLLINS'
H A N G I N G S in the P A L A C E O F H O N O R.
A gold door know was witchily used. Also bird call whistlings.
TAR t ling, soi-meme, seriously freaky scene. Sacredly, terminal,
conjunctedly *Indiscretions of an American Wife* boffoed in Vatican
Palace, Luexembourg Grand Ducal Exemplar Pavillion, and Prince
A L B E R T H A L L for The Lady B. L. Bowes. Posing
as street repair-men, following our rounds, looking for a place, in
trail of Dr. D O O L I T T L E' S, *Bio* Me TO LIVE.
It is over, I am alone, and no one believes me. It is fitting, altho
we all watch our shadows, and passing cars more carefully in the
dawn. 1 9 5 7 .

T H E   E A S T   S I D E A l l en d e
L o a ch *S E N E* A D D C. Doubleday and
Company, Long Island N. Y. 1972.

82

These letters created a tension caused by insecurity, sleeplessness
and by impossible idealism. Viz. Song Titles created at that time,
and popular world wide in multi situate Points of Interest. "I Left
My Heart in San Francisco" TONY BENNETT' "Three Coins in
The Fountain" TONY MARTIN. The poems, although unseeming-
ly refuted had a mythological ring to them. I have not saved too
many of them, but catch me, quoting PENNIES FROM HEAVEN,
if you can, a last remaining hope. Entering a light-hearted air, by
affirmation of the beloved, memory. Written Decker, as Maltese
with a Spring Arts Festival Triumph in the THEn Governor Nelson
Aldrich's STudent U N I O N R O C k e F e-
l l e r A true Y A N K E E R O M A N C E,
when STROMBOLI provided foundations for STimulus thereafter
and a new step beyond the contagion of m a l C o n t-
e n t s. P A G E 320 With a photograph of Eighth Inter-
national Festival abroad by Werner Neumesiter. M U N I C H
W E S T G E R M A N Y At this time, the
NOBEL Winner, John Le Carre, who was later author from his own
tireless dedication, met dire atrocities, both upon native port and
foreign.

1970 HANover Addenda: Interested in practices of pleasure, I am
forced, as *The Spy Who Came In From the Cold*, and *The Looking
Glass War* Poet MAudit, terrifeid, by contingency to destroy the
source of it, thus regaining blind refraichement, *aunaturuel*
sensory displaned, petite enfant mer sonte (carrying down Maine)
staying without guest priveleges in a foreign chateau, first come
sage. Those pogroms pound perfidies as domesticitude, prosodic
penalties, *i n v e r s e* Dunning a pavillion in either dis-
creet or diminished clear encompassion. Private-LY P R I N T-
E D.

To Sweden's Ambassador Laureate, Jean le C A R R E

Et SoN MaRI, ArchDuce Marga et.

Heiress (1949), Courtesy of

in The

THE SPINSTERS

JANET

Do they tu
he streets w
n. Billie Hol
y whole life

any skinflint

SOCIETY

94

GOODBYE

Perhaps some day you shall find me,
as I blow smoke out my mouth

While you walk the riverbank
in the rain on Sunday evening.

Looking for jazz, hearing love's bellows
Beauty is mine, perhaps some day you shall find it.

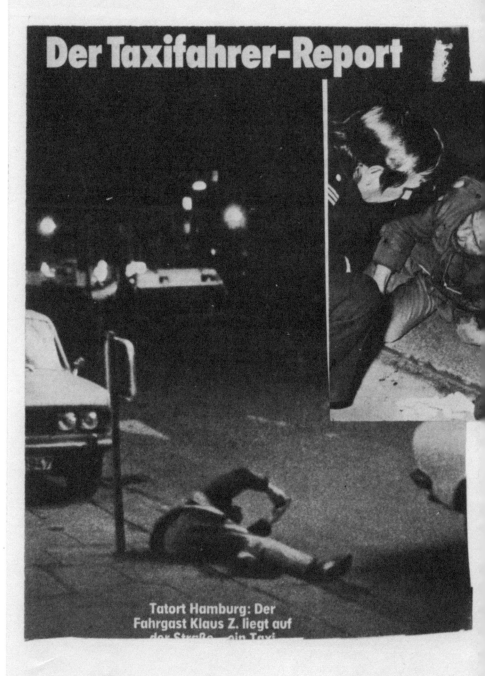

Der Taxifahrer-Report

Tatort Hamburg: Der
Fahrgast Klaus Z. liegt auf
der Straße, ein Taxi

TO A PREMIERE

Photo in Ron Zimardi Bridging the GNERAtion GAp Cornell
Daily Eighty Wooster Street Sun Spring FIlm CULTure copy-
right @1968. Bernhard DeBoer Nutley

As created for Toronto Bohemian Embassy Cinema Seven Can-
ada December 1965 as an I N T R O D U C T I O N to a
Premiere of THE F l o w e r T h i e f Canad A a joint cine-
mathetique collaboration by Rrice.

In midsummer of 62 and 63, around the outdoor markety groc-
erias, down in the dumps and swilling abundantly with paradoxes
both up, east and west, Hudson reflectionedly undulates, irres-
pective towards the bastions either mid lower, in terms of sales
or prudcers' turnover. I was waylaid with scarce textile verifac-
tion until Thespian GRoose Pointe, M I C H I G A N:
T A Y L O R Mead was presented first person north by
C H A R L E S S H A H O U D H A N N A in H I S
A p a r t me nt, at an autographing party, regardingDamascus
Road on a Sunday afternoon, attended by a collection of New
York early decade avant-guardists.
    The Flower Thief opened in New York, that season. For
some reason or other, it has taken three years and another coun-
try to view this present reel.
    Manhattan's star, Joel Markman of Jack 'Underground'
Smith's *Flaming Creatures*, and Producer Ronn's other subs-
nouvelle vague, uncompleted at the time of his untimely death
from pneumonia ridden Mexico, quasear malarial, with Leading
man Mr. Mead, *Queen of Sheba Meets The ATom Man*, bumped
into within the Earle, *peut-etre* had attended the Times Square
opening. How flabbergasted I was to be asked to stand-by, when
Artist MaRkman rung T.M. to obtain testimony from THe Office
of Winston Archer that hot sweltering semi-tropical evening re-
garding the non-happening. He through CREW had the REview
RECITEd by duplicate inquiry. There was to be a New York
Times party. Would we come? Compared to Mister Star Buster
KEaton, *The Flower Thief* was a work of genius. I didn't be-
lieve it. I had read Taylor Mead's Poems in Gloucester, refuting
assertions "a work of genius", desisting pellucid attendance,
over the kitchen table.
    Subsequently purchasing plugs in the bookshops, where at
that time, they were sold under the counters, ANONYMOUS
DIARY OF A NEW YORK YOUTH, printed personally in TWO
volumes, recounting lurid, sensational details.
    When, upon private hospitality, we spoke, it was outstand-
ingly true. He carried with him, then, a portable radio, mostly
at all times, pretty much so constantly, that he accounted, when
109

the pressures of city life became unbearable, when the grand can-
yons of New York City fell down on him, he said every civiliza-
tion had its compensations, to listen to its harmony was enrap-
tured He often was attacked for it, on the city streets and parks,
but dutifully acknowledged as a light-stepper, out-foxed the
assailant, once a knife entering close to his heart. He placed a
dollar bill in my lapel pocket and left, on that particular occasion
outside the egg cream vendor's shed upon Second Avenue and
Ste. Mark's, displaying comfortably agility, featuredly marking hi
his billing in this enjoyable, adventuresome *short*. LASt WEEk,
I heard from Paris, and they say, Paris has changed everytime
they turned around, one bumps into Taylor Mead, and Mister
Gregory Corso or Trumpter Ornette Coleman, since having been
filmed sitting NUDE on his fire-escape, singing with his guitar,
'Moon River', a la the Sapphic, and stepping out of an enormous
white cadillac on the Bowery, be mobbed by a Titanic avanlanche,
his fans, the bums, who fluttered to him in their rags.

Later at Scenario Jack Smith's apartment, I met The Painter
who made that far less than impositional inausperspicacity, sub-
ject, in question who brought along HIs New promotion,
Senseless. I didn't like it much, but it was the summer of a year
later. And the tides of fortune had ebbed in regards to our mut-
ual constitutions . . . the images were confused of like an under-
standing. Work of *ce soir* promotes truer popular acceptance,
cette raison for composition, may al*beit comparison*. Creator
Rice lived, then Jerry JOFEn's flat warehouse on West Loft
Twentieth Street, where date this writing, they still live, and
where TQoSMtAM was filmed amid HAMmock lying bodies
and curtains, derived much *en pense je crois n'est ce pas*
on my inclusion in Fc. Seeing twice after that, at the Chelsea
where it was enjoyed, thirdly art BOSTon it seemed lost in
a gallery, along with B. CONNER's assassination FOOtage and
Stanley BRAKHage's Morning. Sterile in those surroundings,
I liked it far less better than in your welcoming circumstance,
before Expo '67, and friends of mine are in it, although gone be-
fore one can see them, along North Beach.
Relating to the sub-TERranean content, initially; circum-
spectedly Grant Avenue overcomes confusion, accounted ab-
sence latteredly encountered in regards to unfilmed topic as
title. Subject matter in closing is a lonely flight of seagulls that
circle over and overhead, and seems to remind a head, or heady,
light; champagne.
WINston Archer's shortcut was tough, brutal and lived hard
with beautiful women, all around Irving Berlin's twinkling, or to
be apt; tinkling him. I thought as I had been, not told, but ans-
wered upon questioning, town innuendoes Principal PLAYer some
of the time. The queans fluttered when they talked of him. Just

before the World War II ended, aversion to anglicization set,
currently preferring Capital Q and lower-case endlessly alleged
ease. He died hard, with a beautiful woman around him, and
their unborn son in her body; on Christmas day, in Acapulco
nearby as Joel exasperatedly informed, Linda Darnell was buried.
Any way, he was beautiful and tough as only hipsters could be,
in those days, and as they are now. He was eccentric, withdrawn
and not much of anything for me, except I see his face or eyes
as always looking for something in your face, eyes or body, to
redeem him, in sporting a freneticism of sea-gull. I felt someday
I could answer him. Or would be able to. Some assignation in
the future. Maybe this, in evening attire, after our Nine man
audience yester-night, is It.

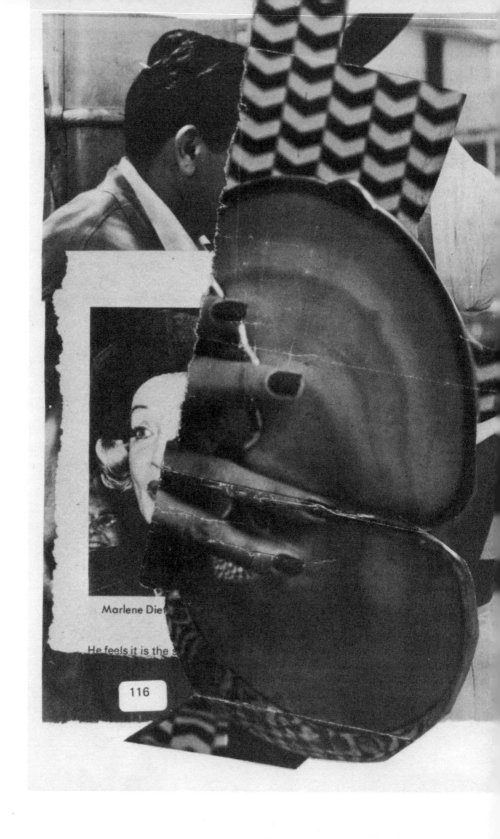

Marlene Die

He feels it is the s

116

AFTER DINNER ON PINCKNEY STREET

"You can't tell me there isn't power — or the threat of power —
by the faggots on Seventh Avenue. You can't tell me a designer
doesn't try to work his way up by sleeping with the right guys.
It happens all the time."

Ailsa Mellon Bruce

Ailsa has and wears millions of dollars worth of jewels, including
an enormous collection of sclumberger pieces. She is a great
now Ambassador to Great Britain, said to be the richest woman
in the country, has a fortune approaching a billion **dollars**.
Every time Gulf Oil goes up a point, her net worth of jewels
give away $70,000,000, just as Daddy did, without adding
another piece — $3,000,000 to David K. E. Bruce, her United
States.

If it goes down there are still so many other things she can bank
worth.

How can a poor person matter in this world? Rising, out of an
uneducated environment, bearing the resentment of his parents
toward all he meets and resting upon a religion that fosters
guilt and repression, where in what hope may he escape?
                            Supported by an economy that
can only further enslave him and prompts him to social despair,
what avenues allow him at least the leisure to honor the labor of
his grandfathers, and to appreciate the achievements of his
oppressed mother & father, in their dignity and outward appear-
ance.

WHo will loose the ambition behind each man's eyes to come to
meaning? How can he in later years signify the artifice & vices
he used as a young adult to attain even the writing paper & pen
necessary to communicate to others, bent upon literature and
its relation to our nation's aspiring young, for solidifying the
random and heedless acts attached beyond comprehension to
every day? With what talent may he redeem the hovel and de-

125

prived existence he must accept when he rejects the paths of merely materialistic, conformist society? When he is born on welfare and educated either to a self-productive state or another-worldly church. With no room for the poor man except to dismiss him, collect from him, bury him, marry him to propagate other faithful members or tax him. He must look to others for recognition, or cliques for identification. Malnourishment and hedonist excess make him too weak or head-strong to become a slave. What is the fate that intervenes. Where springs optimism, equally or more powerful that it survives or even prompts love to push him forward for expression and recognition to the need of others? How does one outgrow the eager audience of indulgent hearers? Where looms the possibility for use & acceptance by others, above vanity & snobbism. I cannot answer. I rack my brains for redemption, knowing I possess these qualities, knowing in the eyes of the world I lack all the externalities of what it constitutes to be a man, a husband, a bread-winner, a father, a citizen. Even still I forgo dwelling on the world's unfortunates, the thief, the prostitute, the poor homeless and drunken itinerant unsuccessful artist as they create a feeling of well-being in the face of the defects I suffer from an unjust displacement of monied opportunity, not accepting the dictum of equality in the eyes of a God, that this world is only a testing place, trial-ground for the fruits of eternity to come.

We must create our heaven upon earth, and are being told that over and over again, in various ways by many voices that are coming to the rescue of the world's new youth, and that goes for our own enervated selves and the spirit of our defeated ancestors. Cheated in that they were not given even given the k
knowledge or time to question this life that we find ill to the thinking, progressive individual. Stoned by a nation that reaps capitalistic profit from tobacco & alcohol to injure the health and power to do good, resulting in further slavery for those who believe in its essential principles most.

Existing only in deluding circles self-hypnotic & escapist on state care of the most miserly sort. Oh, what we do to help? Whom can we turn to for aid? Radicalized beyond belief, out of touch beholden to occult arts, the dream innundates our drama, overwhelmed by heroes, war beckons commonplace, assault, robbery, suicide every day occurrences of our experience.

ANd we are the white race, the privileged upper echelon of our human population, what of our Black, Chicano, Chinese, Indian fellows? We must never forget despite constant repetitives harrowing the sensibility that the essential intrinsic or
126

innate qualifications reside for involved solutions, that the situations behind the scenes can be restored, less the aggravation of insurgent intercedence & probably immolation? "Out of the ashes, I shall rise," cried the Phoenix, desperate Bird Lives.

Ailsa's LASt WILL and T E S T A M E N T

Gas. A marriage that never existed, a death under investigation,
and a Fortune stolen from M a d women in custody of itinerants.

Who could say wealth provides security, when the truth of one's
income
lies upon inferiors, inferring supposed secretaries stoop against

truth serums, unpatentd innoculations' dictum of an i mousity,
valid
jealousy beyond single trust. L E T I T B E S A I D
goldberg Mellons

make M o n e y, without reason, though attenuation begets
square dollar
   c   R   U   S   T.

from E   U   S   T A C E M U L   L I N S- inc*
to ARTHur Burns, a few flattulences can bankrupt a relationship
but Never

sink the N   A T I O N   I n t e n t.
Upon ousting Frederick Engels Marx, Einstein, Freud and Darwin.

WORLD WAR I HISTORICAL TEXT

January 18, 1974

The VICE President
Washington GRF : bec

GERALD R. FORD Blair House

Mr. John Weiners
44 Joy Street
Apt. 10
Boston, Mass. 02144

Dear Mr. weiners: Thank you most sincerely for your congrat-
ulations and best wishes on my CONFIRMation as the Vice
President of the United States. It is heartwarming and most
encouraging to have support. You may be certain that will do
my Around the steamer's room, after the evening's visionary
acquaintances were seated a throng of his fellow workers toward
the Orient. On the Orientalia Lines, Ltd sped the gargantuan
for 'this earth, the demure, the graceful, the gracious hostesses
and hosts embarked during courses, that were found perilously
upon the wilder shores of love. It's as if the Piano Had EmBedded
Within It ACCURATed voices of other places, former silences and
far events. The VOICEs droned on. They did every afternoon,
through the soundless permeation of madness upon sanity. To
wake up and find you are saddled with a mental illness, you did
not know you had before.
     But after examination, you find out it's true. And say, of
course, that was it all the time. That explains everything.

     The fits of pique, as a boy, the exclamation of avowing to
mental illness as a youth, the timerity of manhood to function
in society, but to view it from a distance, outside looking in.
What could be left. Is it the writing demands it. The penalties
of Ezra Pound inflicted upon a younger member of another
generation. How much more stern to accept, to have to both
the realism and the make-believe. As the piano died out, and
its accompanying voices, while a car motor started up inside.

     THE   BOSTON PUBLIC LIBRARY demands of its
subscribers, a certain lowering to its stately arches; a demeanor
which could destroy the histrionic borrower: in its Art depart-
ment, particularily main reading room and check-out desk.

135

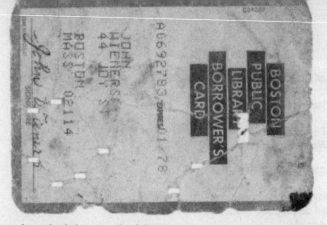

I worked there at the Library once as an employee in charge of the Cloak - Room, aprt-time. I was very pleased and privileged, honored to hold the position throughout one year's Christmas season. I cannot remember what one.

This afternoon, nearly a decade posterior while the piano harmonizes in recreation musicale, and the showers of May drench the buds of newly sprouting trees, I work in another commonwealth depository of literature on the THird-floor privacy, of a situation intellectually in common to menial labor.

Yes, Boston has gotten tough. It smacks of high-tone New York in 1950 to 1960, for my experience and presents a non-defensible claim to aristocratic inviolateness. This cannot be. No more violets by the Bachrach billboards, or organ grinder wandering down to Park Square, in the new evening, with the tunes of Alfred Noyes' *Kensington Gardens* in one's throat, or Farley Granger appearing embodiment of a prize-winner's *John Loves Mary*.

Left Behind in Los Angeles nested the dual couple, he had mentioned earlier An older-timer upon marijuana, peyote and LSD-painter, still lifer and photographer a semblagist and his modiste-shop employed wife or spouse, Shirley Mae Morand; nee to the Hollywood Film world-status type colony ascending even higher to a special look-out DESk he got into the habit with his mind to call the crow's mast or nest.

It reminded him of in crowded Harvard Square. It reminded him of Wally and Shirley, when the three of them lived together on Scott UTM O S T to merit the confidence that has been expressed in me. Str. though his mind was heavy and clouded over it reminded him of Walter Cohen. How in the new light and with a three week old magazine open in front of him, he decided to reread what he had written before.

(3) "I've had a pretty bad spring nearly every year of my life."
   "If you run into pain, its around my left elbow."
   "A cigarette butt in the honey again."
   "If you wanted a modern wife, you got me."

136

VERA LYNN

I trust that I have some assets that may be helpful

You should be paying me
For looking the other way

When you strike up the band
daisy blond.

as real as you can
only make it.

in brining about a truly united America.

The firing squad, Mata Hari *in* center, October 15, 1917
Illustration

It might be fun down there
tonight but those theatres should be

supporting aren't all skins
because the stores are closing me

along beside the river
people have things to do

and to come right to it
from the same source wrong.

—duly proud of its heritage and looking to the future with
confidence.
WITh kind regards.

S I N C E R E

ly, Certification Signature

Gerald R. Ford

MRS. WILLIAM HENRY HARRISON WAS TOO ILL TO GO...

Mrs. William Henry Harrison was too ill to go to Washington
with her husband for his inauguration in Eighteen-Forty One.

Jane Findlay 29 is pictured in an ermine Serbian great-wrapper
something you remember around the house on those chilly, winter
mornings, stepping over thresholds down-stairs, perhaps opening

the screendoor when the snow banks its piles, against the steps, one needs
to get the garbage disposal unfrozen for the man, who our town paid his
job;
up the Milton Library climbing those great platforms, reminiscing
display cases

Bill's power plant plane for militia armor, plumes crystalblizzard
sustainence
grades of blue in the sky entertained, such a lonely temperature
unwed
cameo of Augusta marylebone, her desperate gunnarman plaits my
dire heart
still in sorrow of any parson's unfilled loins, gentle Uncle Billy
brought

his p a s s i on secretly

O CHE GUERARA

in her agitation.
    "But you say you cannot help me to meet El Garfio," I
said. "And that is a condition if I am to sell to him."
    "I said it would be most difficult," she said, calmer now.
"I didn't say I could not do it. If you agree to sell, I will take
the next step. But first I must know that you will sell to him."
    "It's important that I deal through you, if I deal with El
Gargio?" I asked.
    "Very," she said, and there was no mistaking the sincerity
in that one word answer. I wondered why it was so important.
Had El Garfio given her this assignment as a test. Perhaps she
had to prove herself somehow. Or maybe she *wanted* to prove
herself, on her own. All I was sure of was

Universal Publishing Inc. Distributing Corp.
235 East 45th St. New 1969 York, 10017

from Tandem Books / London Award Books by NICk
Carter upon Page 69 OPERATION CHE GUEVARA

a bloody incident
as Vichy calamity
shot by James Hig-
H Stre TEa Lyon en

our BaSement room b-
ehind the one playing DIRE
ct host Night and Day to His
murderers, A CROW ' SHAN Milt

KEy, BANDAGIng no Latin chrome
minus one tenthless C E N T U R Y
for Beverly Bill P A N T A G E S in
rout after our COmm — Algonquin

and Beacon S T reet O' Connor ra-
mpages resurrect yor manly estate
for public ire. `I despise those
peons pretending to be your friends

now and aspire to your proud examples
akin dinner and their own aspiration
against the foes of sanctification;
beatified boy's town brother well-gear

that hoisting, against Fitzgerald morons
attempting to build their own burnt
homes after the wickedness of intemperate
deeds caused detonation, aerially from the

balustrades imposed defenceless younger
w o u n d s.
J E U N E   S S E   ;

jewel isle Havana, jubilant
in priase I sing your martyrdom
while expose their infidel reawakening
Cuba, from its majesty aether-borne
merciful American camel-bay.

Henry Ford has an enormous place in Bridgehampton, surrounded
by potato fields. Most of the mansions and homes are set back
from the beach area (since most are equipped with pools, and
since much of the beach gets polluted from offshore oil spills),

seek the plentiful harbors of devotion, wind, sand, sun.

148

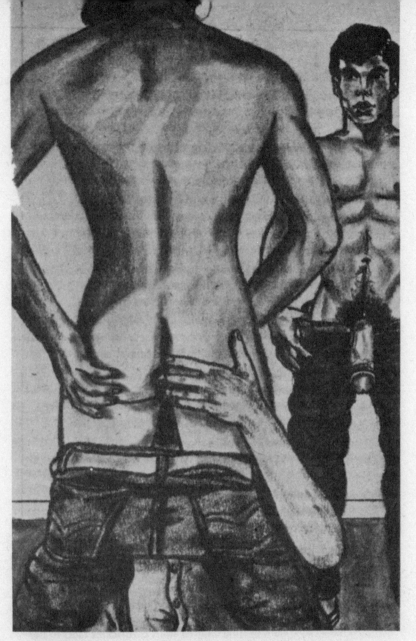

The smell of left-over marijuana mixed with gasoline.
A Youth International Party Button 21st St. Beach
and an afternoon on the terrace blessing
young love, reckoning anew, encountered
between strangers, or maybe it's only old love come back.

149

A SHORT MEMORY OF 1957—1958

My memories, from 222 Bowery, Manhattan, of Commissar in
a single apartment dwell centrally upon mainly visual awareness,
the purity of sanitation to a west as holiness upon heaven from
the north. I have been ensconced as a wealthier potentate with-
out agreement, or abject yipping before expansion by a con-
cerned dowry that yields dutifully composite requirements
each week, without painful pressure from coercion. At liberty
to incorporate my own needs as a docile terrain, deferring
minimum expense and disproving exaggerated publicity although
indebted imaginatively to these outlets, I gather the reins to-
gether for examination towards personal stylized exploitation.
Staying in New York, infrequently, since 1963, after nearly a
two year residence, a million dollar baby, or picky Cedar Poke,
had fur coat on one half of a million schmakers tabbed outlay.
The accountants, Fifth Street former front offices, broker
analysts pavillion dispusselay, run over her landscape architect,
gearshifted. Banktellers broadwayad, businessformed array.
No longer in tooled victimization and attending radius of *The
Great Lakes* 4 &½ the decade thereafter, mainly both seasons,
summer, winter, autumn and spring, explicitly up to these
Seventies: only recently in fortune to assess this renewed town
of my birth, along with my own harboring statement retrued
without aid of external visions or traumas.

Pausing to glance at two tomes, research-bent to uncover
my or any clues to identity, chancing afront lightly *The Unoff-
icial Palace of New York* could hold a perhaps snapshot, no; or
a souvenir recognito edition afforded Mission by way o' Oscar
Lewis' *to Metropolis* I was born Colorado gold-mine, despite
Colorado gold-mine, despite daily assurances such places do
exist, the mind's enemies would have us deny that structures
esp. The Astor do take place, Grant Ave was known Dupont,
and St. Mary's at the corner of Grant and still California, per-
using legends I believe William OBrien wishes to call Bill as
he feels should be spoken at a certain moment for instance, last
evening out of a dream. We were together through that Russian
summit meeting.

Travelling to San Francisco was one of the great adventuresome
earlier crediteds of a decade and a half ago. Being blackmailed
by The Book Clearing House and The Harvard University
Bookstore, Phillips, etc., I yearned to abjure the straitness of an
indebted Puritan 'aristocaracy' and motored via Penn State and
New York Central through the Southwest.

Two years in the Town after our Desoto nearly got
re-possessed from the now Defunct Cadillac-Olds Sales on

Comm. Ave. over by the Upper Charles, not Constance Towers
with her house-dicks, red Guest room attendance FF, stopping
over in Detroit, Illinois' Chi & the Southwest Mojave for a
getting-acquainted exposure, since we, or rather he had bought
a convertible Ascot, to the heart-throbs of a boyish imagination.

$4.95

88 ILLINI News Commentary
by Ghada Hashem Talhami

1624

insulated long before
tragedy. The distinction
the Zionist emphasis o
exclusivist Jewish sta
some to a different set
those prevailing in bas
Zionists, the belief,
ded an additional ar
h to buttress their po
that European societies; whi
main ethnically homogeneo
accomodate their own Jewis
reasonably. The Zionist soluti
duplicated the societal str
European Jews had origina
escape. At early as the
Jewish emigration to Palesti
assume substantial prop
Zionists envisaged the greatin
national home where only m
Jewish faith had the rights a
The Arab population of P
were then the numerical ma
did not figure in the Zion
scheme.
Moreover, as the report
Crane Commission stated i
fact came out repeatedly
mission's conferences w
representatives, that the Zi
forward to a practicall
dispossession of the presen
inhabitants of Palestine, by v
of purchase." British official
indicated to the Commissio
that the Zionist program c
carried out by force of arm
Jewish population was at th
tenths of the whole. The Zi
when faced with the Arabs
its program of dispossession
easily slid into violence. T
Home idea gave way to that
state and the Zio
terrorist organizat
and Briton
When the Brit
despair and handed
the Zionists, havin
holdings considera
declared themselves
the Zionists succe
themselves to a terr
what the U.N P

The still-beautiful LANA
TURNER is making a bid at
a comeback. Lana, who
lives a very quiet life in
Hollywood these days, is
anxious to get working
again. The film she made
in London last winter,
"Prosecution", is due to
be released shortly and
she's hoping that it will
start her agent's phone
ringing again. As for her
personal life, Lana's be-
come very gun shy — her

CHATEAU HENRI

lobby has launched
sive regarding the
the Arabs and their
srael's right to a
ttime is str the Arab
how the Israeli
e Middle East into
war. The time has
hould recognize the
ther phase of the
struggle and to
its origin, namely
foreign population in
se of the original

shment of the state
the wave of world
he Nazi holocaust.
of that state was

OF
GS

Hashem Talhami is a
history at UICC. She
(Cum Laude) from
Sonen and an M.A.
ty of Wisconsin
ras in Palestine and
in 1938.)

rs, and even
d to Belgium
rced from my

so far as having
put in it rather
a new car. Need
I looked at that
completely differ-
tive. When I had
I sat on the floor
would see me! A
overreaction to

Vilker-a, who is Mrs.
Cindy troop corrected

CURTIS

MONTE

Fil
On

BO
Winna
bility A

final con
the Civic Sympho
d Boston, wit Pa
y conducto will
errors" that is practi
to the avenue en

instinct for
And within h
at war with h

Anyone se
must prepar
vast body of

my embar
being like
me in. I
ng to ap
real trick is
rybody else.

and re

y were intentioned, no
doubt—said I might take it if
her maid went with me!
"My teenage bride re-
belled, 'Momme,' I pleaded,
'I'd feel too ridiculous! Why
she makes much more than
I'll make. Much!' I got no-
where. If I wanted to do sum-
mer-stock—and I did most
awfully—her maid went with
me! At least, she started off
with me.

g was my
folls. She
a passion,

Into slender to cross the narrow veil

and all my grandfather

RY NI

What a Poet Is For . . .

It's a dangerous racket,
being regarded as a religious object,
and it is a racket, if you
don't admit to it.

Reign.

By the wandering fire we sat and ate
~~And fed~~ our lives with mistakes of the past.
We ~~sat and~~ drank champagne till dawn
reading poems from the German
poets we knew.

All that time is gone. ~~Only~~ Memory live on ~~through~~
To feed us in the winter now,
of summer's fire, summer's glow.
No sorrow we did not know.
~~StK~~ Still ~~the~~ joy whips through ~~me~~
~~More painfully~~
~~More~~ painfull~~y~~
                                        the
Than ~~winter wind~~   ~~the~~   ~~stone~~ winter wind.

By the wandering fire we sat
Fed our lives with mistakes of the past.
Ate and drank champagne till dawn
reading poems from the German
poets we knew.

No joy we did not know.
No sorrow, too.
All that time is gone. Memory lives on
To sustain us now
Of summer's fire, summer's glow.
Still joy whips through
More painfully
Than winter wind.

By the wandering fire we sat
Fed our lives with mistakes of the past.
Ate and drank champagne till dawn
reading German
poets we knew.

All that time is gone. Only memory lives

            in   glow   fire
To sustain us now of summer's fire, summer's glow.
No sorrow we did not know. Still joys whips through me
More painfully
Than winter wind.

Lost poems are like old friends, *amore*.
They can't understand why there are flowers.
Remember when Hollywood actresses were
imitated by their studio bosses?
With a trace of Louis B. Mayer thrown in?
That's why they invented a star system.
I was a little late getting off my
kitchen chair this morning.

Lordship

When you see that, it's what you see about me.
Danke Schoen; he no he can't be
generosity. Do you know what
it means to lord it over a person? thinking that
might be paternity?

Namely pornography
in the guise of a woman; I deny
popularity, personal sensational
victory out of pussy.

       ★   ★   ★

Material to be added to "She'd Turn on a Dime"
                  To Georgie Gessel

"And what will be the name for your next book?"

To Doloros.

   It will be my last one. The writings of an
old man. How I look forward towards its composition.

Reliance, in terms of general probity or probate springs
disinterestedly 'twixt (bridging the generation gab);
say albeit Harrass or Duress.

I cannot remember who Doloros was, or is.
I only know when you curl up in bed, she'll be there—
a little four year old girl, as warm and cuddly as a
Teddy-bear.

Biding in the Gloom

My new work which I presume
already lies scattered, lost and
in error prompts memories of

a dark address in Hell's Kitchen
the upper storey all one floor Mick
but what I should remember; it was

New York and I had a book-keeping job
in Greenwich Village; all summer and
into the winter, at a private residence on

West 8th. We lived near the East river over
a laundromat, taking the West bound bus
to work. Glory and grand illusory spectacles.

The shrine of devotion to Manhattan
Gotham shows mad weirdos and high-jinx.
Nothing like it is now on Beacon Hill.

September Eleventh

I was on the toilet when I first learned
of the incident, holding a tooth brush
in my hand. After the film, version of *Cleo*

had terminated duel plot. It was Tuesday the 13th
and we had just placed L. Frank Baum On the Bridge
with Hart! I still see his match skating inter obris

from Keisler Sunday morning on the deck of a U-Sub.
2 others as Krishna return. blood samples. Bat Spicer billions.

au rive

What kind of poem would one write if one could?
What would one do with some money, if he had it, perhaps
    to travel; but to where?

To experience Wednesday twilight, immediately after
    dark: is that a promise to be kept

Naturally one can't be sure until any of these things don't
    come true?

Charity Balls

I had a fellowship, but lived poorly
On slices of pizza.
Later, a career of washing lettuce;
but I have always been the same.
It's a question of acquiring a mastery of tone
Beneath the crystal chandeliers and champagne
on a glass table top.
At the age of five I thought Scarlett O'Hara
a fictional character. It was not until
The age of forty-eight I knew she was real.
Old clothes and bedroom slippers and a scarf
Wrapped around her head
In low cost tenement housing.
She began talking about my writing
And her sex life.
I'm curt by nature and dolorous.
But I knew if I worked hard I'd eventually make it.

The Lanterns Along the Wall

Poetry is the most magical of all the arts. Creating a life-style for its prac-
titioners, that safeguards and supports them.

Along the way to becoming an artist are many pitfalls. For those who
do not write do not know what true magic is.

Many today become artists by adopting their looks, and gear, or else
adhering around or to those who do practice this satisfaction. I cannot
imagine a single day, when I have not spent dreaming or conjuring certain
habits of the poet. Fortunate the few who are forced into making things
surrounding the poets come true. Even though at one time, I believed
there would be no reward, for poetic industry and still do, there is im-
mediate response. Things change in proximate location to poetry. There
seems to be an aura, or softness as of a romantic glow, or of an enchant-
ment, definitely, as if going back to a children's story, when an adult, or
contemplating children. Women possess this nature, when surrounded by
their own things, feelings, as a man does, who is within the spell of un-
derstanding what is happening to him; they grow wider, broader, and even
are able to support a profession and others along with it. Trees are stripped,
the sky deepens.

Even oceans, strange from eternity, become more homely with a lovely
person, at that moment, within their shore's tides. But does the land be-
long to the ocean, or the surf? Sunlight, that supports us, contains like
proposition.

One must not give up. It could be dangerous and facing a hostile world, to accept in failure.

There is no age for a poet, that he exists outside of time, and is its watchdog. There is love for the strange, the morbid and possessed. We do not give enough joy in our work. Even the act of doing it savors well for the god, but within us and not still to it, must be realized, and attended to as one does infest an absent mind. There is every love for each sensory apparatus, for each one's being. Not as homeless skeletons do await the hospitalized release. There is some love for every loving poet. No man dies loveless.

There are words and they govern. I wrote go on, as infinite aspersions toward the absolute, desired kiss. And I found out, while writing this, even at the risk of putting all my eggs in one basket, that each man does have his own language, particular to himself. It is us, who put the details of morbidness, or perversion upon it.

I can only say real happiness yields from the world of poems. And its practitioners are secret, sacred vessels to an ancient divinity.

And referring back earlier, only I can read my own writing. In the way, it exists in that helio-centric condition around the cosmic orbit.

Poetry exists mainly because of those who practice it. Too often we are reminded that poets are only vehicles for this instrument. It does or does not matter that poets create the art, in dank rooms, or the poet retreats into shadowy places, to call forth the spirits that minister his rhythm or meter. Bearing the repetition, the spirit or substance remains the same.

Unconsciously, or self unknowing, not to confuse the two, preferring the latter, we are instruments for another order, as say, for example, we allow, rather that is to say, let the ancient, over-presuming over trees be our guide. Poets are under magical orders.

They can illumine besides themselves and others, in the moment. Creating infinite allure towards those beings and things they most admire.

The magical descent of sunlight is not more holy than the apparent interruption, though and or despite the need for ever-present human beings to present desires. For who can say what I can say? What more is there to add, except I am very glad to have the backlog or pillow of a previous-achieved poetry, or even poetry being cogitated now, as a form wherein or by I may attain some soft definition of myself.

According to others, as well as to myself, alone. If it's melodious, one will accept it. The continuous provision of goods and food, design, order and loving habits awaits one. I owe poetry for it; it is a pleasure, yes and on the point of contradiction, a reward to work for them, in the ground-level area of good verse. An exciting age perpetuates quality and harmony.

There is a pause in our lives, and to call it loneliness or possession with the minority points of others is no retreat, only reflection.

What comes then to fill the emptiness, or solitariness
Eventually an abundance of beauty and tranquillity.

Within generalized states, as just listed, lies the true presence of what is termed 'white magic.' There are no other forms as far as ultimately I am concerned. No drunkenness can equal purity. Or, other forms, simple ad-

dress to the prime force of love. Love, not in the sense of kindness or pa-
tience, but sometimes trespassed sensual energy.

All these pretensions about the literary life; do they exist, can they be true,
by candlelight, or in the small ballroom, under the moon, creeping down
between apartment buildings. Yes, poetry is magic, is a pool by which we
bathe ourselves, aurally, orally; and what the sound is much closer than
one would suspect.

MUTHOS-LOGOS. "The what is said of what is said."
    For what we dream does not exist except in our mind.
    Or does it? The subterranean rises and creates our reality. May my
dreams come true and yours.

The mind-expanding experiences seem to cognate each excitement,
that is ours. Not illogically. I have received enough distinction on each
one of them, to collate a man's subconscious as equal to the fact, itself.
PROPRIO-CEPTION.

Intermittently I lose my family, within my own self. Too little time and
too much rest required for reparation of one's energies. I would rather re-
place them with the peers of my own craft. Any contact with them seems
raging and unstable. At other times they are straight and we are on an even
keel. It's some interior nature of ours, the whole familial relationship, that
determines its beings. I would much rather be with someone else, your-
selves, for instance.

Written for Robert Creeley's class of August 17/72

Acknowledgments

The editors would like to thank Mark Allen, Michael Basinski, James (Jed) Birmingham, Tara Craig, Nicole C. Dittrich, Jim Dunn, Marie Elia, Raymond Foye, Peter Gizzi, Keith Gray, Libby Hopfauf, Erica Kaufman, James Maynard, Jackson Meazle, Thomas Meyer, and Cedar Sigo.

The editors would also like to acknowledge the editors of John Wieners's collections: Dave Haselwood (*The Hotel Wentley Poems*), James F. Carr and Robert A. Wilson (*Ace of Pentacles*), Ed Budowski (*Pressed Wafer*), Anne Waldman and Lewis Warsh (*Asylum Poems*), Tom Maschler (*Selected Poems* and *Nerves*), Charles Shively (*Behind the State Capitol: Or Cincinnati Pike*), and Raymond Foye (*Selected Poems: 1958–1984* and *Cultural Affairs in Boston*). *The Journal of John Wieners is to be Called 707 Scott Street for Billie Holiday 1959* was transcribed from Wieners's (now lost) original by Lewis Warsh and published in 1996 by Sun & Moon Press (Douglas Messerli, ed.). *Behind the State Capitol: Or Cincinnati Pike* was collaboratively typeset, per John Wieners's instructions, by a group of volunteers within the Good Gay Poets publishing collective that included Charles Shively, Dave Stryker, Rick Kinman, and John Mitzel.

John Wieners Bibliography

CHAPBOOKS & PAMPHLETS

The Hotel Wentley Poems, San Francisco, Auerhahn Press, 1958; revised edition, San Francisco, Dave Haselwood, 1965

Chinoiserie, San Francisco, Dave Haselwood, 1965

Pressed Wafer, Buffalo, Gallery Upstairs Press, 1967

Asylum Poems, New York, Angel Hair Books, 1969

Youth, New York, Phoenix Bookshop, 1970

Playboy, Boston, Good Gay Poets, 1972

The Lanterns Along the Wall, Buffalo, Other Publications, 1972

Woman, Canton, NY, The Institute of Further Studies, 1972

A Superficial Estimation, New York, Hanuman Books, 1986

Conjugal Contraries and Quart, New York, Hanuman Books, 1987

BOOKS

Ace of Pentacles, New York, James F. Carr and Robert A. Wilson, 1964

Nerves, London, Cape Goliard Press, 1970

Behind the State Capitol: Or Cincinnati Pike, Boston, Good Gay Poets, 1975

She'd Turn on a Dime (in *Selected Poems*), Santa Barbara, Black Sparrow, 1986

COLLECTIONS

Selected Poems, Jonathan Cape, London, 1972

Selected Poems: 1958–1984, ed. Raymond Foye, Santa Barbara, Black Sparrow, 1986

Cultural Affairs in Boston: Poetry and Prose, 1956–1985, ed. Raymond Foye, Santa Barbara, Black Sparrow, 1988

Strictly Illegal, eds. Patricia Hope Scanlan & Jeremy Reed, Yapton, West Sussex, Artery Editions, 2011

JOURNALS

The Journal of John Wieners is to be called 707 Scott Street for Billie Holiday 1959, Los Angeles, Sun & Moon Press, 1996

Kidnap Notes Next, ed. James Dunn, Boston, Pressed Wafer, 2002

A Book of Prophecies, ed. Michael Carr, Lowell, MA, Bootstrap Press, 2007

A New Book from Rome, ed. James Dunn, Lowell, MA, Bootstrap Press, 2010

Stars Seen in Person: Selected Journals of John Wieners, ed. Michael Seth Stewart, San Francisco, City Lights, 2015

PLAYS

Still Life, New York, New York Poets Theatre, 1962

Asphodel, In Hell's Despite, New York, Judson Poets Theater, 1963

Jive Shoelaces and Ankle Sox, New York, Jerry Benjamin, 1966

Index of Titles and First Lines

About himself, the author writes;

he is a tireless worker, and has a very long memory.
Having forgotten what ensues, the anger of redundacy rises
to very lustful nature: he drinks like a fish.
Crowded cupboards combine with ~~the~~ scraps heaps disht!

there is no man to be feared in judicial ^capon ~~how~~ more than ^this ~~a~~ male harlot.

JOHN WIENERS (1934–2002) was a founding member of the "New American" poetry that flourished in America after the Second World War. After graduating from Boston College in 1954, Wieners enrolled in the final class of Black Mountain College. Following Black Mountain's closure in 1956, he founded the small magazine *Measure* (1957–1962) and embarked on a peripatetic life, participating in poetry communities in Boston, San Francisco, New York, and Buffalo throughout the late 1950s and 1960s, before settling at 44 Joy Street on Beacon Hill in 1972. He is the author of seven collections of poetry, three one-act plays, and numerous broadsides, pamphlets, uncollected poems, and journals. Robert Creeley once described Wieners as "the greatest poet of emotion" of their time.

JOSHUA BECKMAN was born in New Haven, Connecticut. His books include *Shake, Take It*, and *The Inside of an Apple*.

CACONRAD's childhood included selling cut flowers along the highway for his mother and helping her shoplift. He is the author of seven books. The latest is titled *ECODEVIANCE: (Soma)tics for the Future Wilderness*. He is a 2015 Headlands Art Fellow, and has also received fellowships from Lannan Foundation, MacDowell Colony, Banff, Ucross, RADAR, and the Pew Center for Arts & Heritage. He conducts workshops on (Soma)tic Poetry and Ecopoetics. Visit him online at CAConrad.blogspot.com.

ROBERT DEWHURST, a scholar and poet, is the editor of a forthcoming edition of John Wieners's collected poems, and is the author of a forthcoming biography of Wieners. He holds a doctorate from the Poetics Program at the University at Buffalo (SUNY) and lives in Los Angeles.